Art and Soul

Art and Soul

Generating Missional Conversations
with the Community through
the Medium of Art

Michelle Sanders

Foreword by
Reggie McNeal

WIPF & STOCK · Eugene, Oregon

ART AND SOUL
Generating Missional Conversations with the Community through
the Medium of Art

Wipf and Stock
An Imprint of Wipf and Stock Publishers
199 W. 8th Ave., Suite 3
Eugene, OR 97401

www.wipfandstock.com

ISBN 13: 978-1-62564-469-5

Manufactured in the U.S.A.   09/09/2014

Dedication

This book is dedicated to all who step out of their comfort zones to reach out to those within their communities. Special thanks to my husband, Mick, who constantly stands with me through my harebrained schemes. To my children, Orien and Daniel, Levi and Rhyanon, and Michael and Nicole who all involve themselves with these schemes in many ways. Thanks to my wonderful artist friend Jennifer Koch who continues to explore new options with me. To Mike Leshon who has been willing to take a risk to make a difference in the lives of prisoners. To my friends who have involved themselves on so many levels, Lynn Moresi, Grant and Trudy Buchanan, Anthony and Vicki Ware. Our Art and Soul facilitators, Nicole Sanders, Kelly Goeby, Orien Westendorp, Cymone Levell, Jamie and Candi Toll, John Koch, Paul and Lauren Ward, Samantha Brown and Coby Jager and to the Kaleidoscope community for being willing to be a place that accepts and embraces those who would not normally step inside the doors of a church.

So from now on we regard no one from a worldly point of view. Though we once regarded Christ in this way, we do so no longer. Therefore, if anyone is in Christ, the new creation has come: The old has gone, the new is here! All this is from God, who reconciled us to himself through Christ and gave us the ministry of reconciliation: that God was reconciling the world to himself in Christ, not counting people's sins against them. And he has committed to us the message of reconciliation. We are therefore Christ's ambassadors, as though God were making his appeal through us. We implore you on Christ's behalf: Be reconciled to God.

—1 CORINTHIANS 5:16–20

Contents

Foreword

I REMEMBER WELL THE first time it really came home to me the importance of art in faith formation. It was during my first visit to York Minster in northern England many years ago now. This Gothic cathedral boasts the best collection of medieval stained glass art work in the world. I was fortunate enough to be touring the church when most of the other two million visitors who drop in each year were doing something else. So I had time to sit for a good period in front of the largest window and take it in.

At some point I suddenly realized that I was "reading" the Bible. From left to right, row upon row, each of the dozens of frames of stained glass recounted each significant story in the Book, from the creation in Genesis to the depiction of the eschaton in the post-historical kingdom of heaven fully come. Each picture served like an icon on a computer screen. Behind each frozen representation was an entire narrative. The stories of Adam, Noah, Abraham, Moses, Joseph, David, Elijah, John the Baptist, Peter, Paul, John, Jesus—along with episodes of dry ground crossings, battles and births, miraculous deliverances and death—are all chronicled in this massive window. This art form of sand, pigment, glaze, metal, and imagination had preserved and passed along the faith for hundreds of years for the worshippers who passed through this sacred space. Those same worshippers, who could not do their "daily Bible readings" (after all, they probably couldn't read and almost certainly did not own a Bible) could in this spot rehearse the history of God's dealings with humanity.

Of course in York and in all other centers of Christendom people "went to church" for centuries. They showed up for worship services to sing, hear teaching, and participate in the sacraments. This is how they learned the backstories to the illuminated images suspended in glass art. They had to "be there" to get it.

The challenge of communicating the faith today is profoundly different. We have entered a post-congregational era in Western culture. People are much less likely to attend worship services and religious celebrations. For a variety of reasons they are less susceptible to being congregationalized in their spiritual journey. Perhaps their employment doesn't recognize Sunday as a day off. Those who labor in hospitality and healthcare industries or first responders along with many retailers, don't have the luxury of closing their doors on Sunday to enjoy a day of worship. (Imagine a hospital or police station or a restaurant—egads!—posting a sign on their door: "closed for church.") Even more people, many with spiritual ambitions, simply won't match their life rhythms to the rhythm of congregational life, repeating the same religious activities every seven days, fifty-two weeks a year. The bottom line: people aren't "there" anymore to get it (teaching, sacraments, etc.).

So how do we engage people with God's story who aren't and won't "come to church?"

Art is the answer. The stained glass has to leave the building. Okay, we can leave it there for those who still worship in that space or buy museum tickets to look at it. But the art has to go—onto the streets—to people who don't know the Story. We must find new ways of engaging spiritual beings with the good news of the kingdom of God right where they already work, play, go to school, recreate, reside—right in the middle of their lives.

Enter Michelle Sanders. I met Michelle when she took a class I teach at Fuller Seminary as part of her doctoral work. To say that she is both high-energy and super-relational would be an understatement (she had the class doing Tim Tam slams by midweek). To say that she has a heart for and as big as the world would be about right. Combine all of this with her love of art and appreciation for its capacity to reveal and to connect with the human soul and what do you get? A missional strategist who sees art as spiritual conversation.

Thankfully Michelle has written this fine volume to let us all in on her insights. You will not find in these pages suggestions on how to have stilted and awkwardly artificial conversations (the one my tribe taught me growing up—"do you know you are going to hell and fry like sausage?" was just a non-starter). What you will find is thoughtful reflection, borne of real-life experience, on how to have artful conversations that help people discover and experience the life God has in mind for them.

So, come along. Grab your art and soul. Let's go outside and play!

Reggie McNeal

Best-selling author, The Present Future
and Missional Renaissance

INTRODUCTION

Connecting with People's Stories

IN 2009, WHILE VISITING America as part of my doctoral studies at Fuller, I realized that the vacation was all about me: my studies, my ministry and visiting my friends. I recognized that I needed to do something that would be of interest and involve my husband, Mick. That's when I had a brain wave. I decided that we should hire a Harley and ride across America.

This idea turned into the most amazing journey. As often happens with my bright ideas, once begun to form they take on a life of their own. This motorbike ride quickly turned into "The American Harley Tour." I set up a Facebook page where the mission became: We are off to America to find a hillbilly with a gun, some moonshine and a banjo. Before long we had around 250 followers, journeying with us across the country. Each day as I awoke I would discover more challenges for us to attempt posted on the Facebook page. We were challenged to hula-hoop in the foyer of a hotel, to dress up in all kinds of weird and wonderful clothes and visit some amazing places.

My favorite challenge, although a little scary, was: "Go and get yourself photographed with a real bike gang." One day in Oklahoma, we were at a gas station and I looked up and saw two patched bikies. With great excitement I ran over to them and began to blurt out in my best Aussie accent, "G'day, we're from Australia and we're on a mission to find a hillbilly with a gun, some moonshine and a banjo, and part of our challenge is to get ourselves photographed with a real bike gang and you look like a bike gang, can I get a photograph with you?" They both looked at me like I was from another planet. I think they had a little difficulty understanding me as well. My husband joined us, looking really concerned. But the more I talked I could see the bikers were warming to me. So I pushed on. Mick was telling me later that a lot of bikers don't want to be photographed. I hadn't considered that at the time.

So the bikers graciously allowed me to photograph myself with them, turning them and posing them in several ways. The more we talked the more relaxed it became. Finally they told me that they were about to go on a bike run, and invited us back to the clubrooms to meet the rest of the gang. I immediately answered, "Yes! We would love to!" Mick did not look so sure. However, we followed them back to the clubrooms. I was in my element. There was a whole gang there that I was able to take out and pose and photograph myself with.

We began to talk about who they were and their club—BACA: Bikers Against Child Abuse. I had never heard of them before and was amazed at their mission. They would camp out around houses of children who were being abused and would put the heavies on the perpetrators. They would go to court as support if a child was afraid to give evidence. The more I spoke to these men the more I liked who they were. They told me that there are a couple of chapters of the BACA group in Australia. Once I returned to our hotel that evening I emailed the group in Australia and we have since gone on a couple of runs with them.

The big thing I realized is that these guys would never step foot inside a church. And unless we go into our communities and connect with those outside of our four walls we will never get to share the love that Jesus has for these people. Sitting in our buildings calling people to come into our churches not only is ineffective, it was not the mandate given. We are the ones told to "go into all of the world and share the good news."

In 2011, when I was again visiting America for study and vacation, I decided to create some interest in the holiday. Everything seemed to be so dull after our great American Harley Tour. So I decided this time I needed to come up with something that would cause us to meet people, engage with their stories and look for ways to generate some missional conversations. The end result of this became the American Painting Tour. How this worked was I would look out for someone on my travels and ask if I could paint them. Every person that I asked to paint agreed to the request.

The first person I met was a man who called himself Sergio, "The Sexican Mexican." Sergio appeared to be the archetype of a shallow sitcom television show. You could hear Sergio before you could see him and he seemed to polarize those in the room. I could tell some were thinking what a lovely friendly man, but others were thinking, I wish he would just quiet down. However, I was fascinated with him. When I asked if I could paint him, he quickly agreed. I told him that he needed to take the time to consider the request, as the catch was, that when I painted him I also wanted his story. Sergio had no hesitations. I was expecting to receive a story telling me that he was the Sexican Mexican, the greatest lover in history or some shallow story about his life.

What ensued was fascinating. He began to tell me that he grew up with a sense of shame because of who he was. He was ashamed of his heritage. He continued to relate that his mother died when he was fourteen. His father was a very harsh man and so Sergio left home at fifteen. He had always felt guilty that he left his younger brother at home. His eyes filled with tears as he told me that he was reconciled with his father after many years and three years previously he sat with him on his deathbed. I was astounded at how open Sergio was and could not get over how quickly we went from a very shallow conversation to something of great depth.

What I discovered as I met people each day on that vacation, was that they were happy to share their stories. I decided to add in a further clause to the Painting Tour. I would tell the person that

I met, that it would take me two to four weeks to paint them and as I paint, I pray. I asked them what would they like me to pray for them during that time. In every case, the person was really moved by this. They openly told me things that I could pray for. I have kept in touch with many of the subjects. What this has shown me is that when I take an interest in people and ask about their lives, they have been willing to allow me in. Not only this, they are happy for me to pray for them and this has given rise to me being able to share missional conversations on many occasions with people who would never enter a church building.

I am currently working on a painting project with another artist friend where we will continue to do this in our own community. Wendy works at my local café. She makes fantastic coffee and is so warm and friendly. I was sitting watching her recently as I was waiting for my next appointment, wondering how to go to the next level of conversation with her. Then the thought struck me, Wendy could be my first subject. So I approached Wendy asking if I could paint her. She was surprised, and not sure how to respond, but after agreeing, we began to talk about her life. I took Wendy out to another café for coffee and she began to share her story of anorexia, divorce and other things that I will not share here. I asked Wendy what I could pray for. As she shared it was a really touching moment. This conversation moves us to a place where God begins to work. I have since been praying for her and God has been responding to my prayer. It's amazing what is happening in her life.

So this project that I am continuing to work on will consist of twenty-four portraits. I am working on twelve and my artist friend, Jennifer Koch,[1] will also paint twelve people. I am currently excited imagining opening night. The first night will be invitation only, the subjects, their friends and family, as well as members of my faith community, Kaleidoscope, who are currently praying for the people we are painting. I am envisioning these people walking in and seeing their portrait, we will have their story written on a plaque beneath the painting. Below that will be another plaque

1. www.jenniferkoch.webs.com.

with the prayer that we have been praying for them. I expect this will be quite confronting for our subjects, but I believe that as they see their painting and look at what we have prayed for, that God will have answered these prayers, maybe not in ways that they may have expected, but in the way that God does that. This will be a culmination of several conversations with our new friends and I am excited to see where God will take this.

The imago Dei is a concept that is found in three Old Testament scriptures.[2] In essence it reveals that humanity is created in the image of God. This means that every person, regardless of their function or standing, has inherent value just because they exist and are created in the likeness of their Creator. Jesus condenses the Decalogue into just two commandments: love God and love people.[3] This demands an action or response, particularly from the church.

Karl Barth writes that the missio Dei emphasizes that God is the initiator of his mission to redeem every person in the world through his people, the church. He sent his Son for this purpose and now he sends the church into the world with the message of the gospel for the same purpose.[4] Bosch writes that the classical doctrine on the missio Dei is a Trinitarian view, with God the Father sending the Son and the Son sending the Spirit, this was expanded to include another sending of the Holy Spirit sending the church into the world. He continues that the church exists because there is mission, not vice versa. To participate in mission is to participate in the movement of God's love toward people, since God is a fountain of sending love.[5] If this fountain is only contained within the church it becomes a cistern and the water is restricted.

Guder concurs, stating that mission is not merely an activity of the church but the result of God's initiative, rooted in God's purposes to restore and heal creation, and it is the central biblical theme describing the purpose of God's action in human history.

2. Gen 1:27–28; 5:1–3; 9:6.
3. Mark 12:30–31.
4. Sanders, *Mission of God and the Local Church*, 24.
5. Bosch, *Transforming Mission*, 390.

God's mission is calling and sending us, the church of Jesus Christ, to be a missionary church in our own societies, in the cultures in which we find ourselves.[6] Alan Hirsch takes this one step further stating that not only a product of that mission but is obligated and destined to extend it by whatever means possible.[7]

This world is broken. It is filled with death, disease, pain, rejection, oppression and disappointment. People are hurting and confused. Running "Art and Soul,"[8] a ten-week course teaching people who suffer depression and anxiety to paint, I constantly see these things deeply embedded in people's lives. The mission of the church is to embody a message of hope, one of connection, reconciliation and relationship with the Creator, the one who gives purpose and meaning. To do this it is essential for the church to go to the people, not wait for them to recognize that they have a need and come into the church buildings. Those who are wounded rarely see God as the hope of the world and more rarely see the church as offering this hope. The more common perception is that the church is the one that brings judgment and condemnation. Therefore, it is essential to really look at God's message for those in pain and struggling, but further, how to communicate this message. If we are huddled in our church buildings we are not participating in the missio Dei. While the gathering together for worship, communion, teaching and fellowship is important, there needs to be more.

"Art and Soul," part of my doctoral studies at Fuller Theological Seminary, is a course that I developed to deliberately reach out to our world. It is one way to connect with many people who are in pain who would never enter a church. Katrina's daughter had died one week before she turned eighteen. Twenty-one days after her daughter died, her mother suddenly passed away. Katrina was left devastated. She had no desire, interest or even concept that church would be a place of comfort. Katrina found solace in God through connecting in an "Art and Soul" course. We have had continued

6. Guder, *Missional Church*, 5.

7. Hirsch, *Forgotten Ways*, 82.

8. www.artandsoul.org.au.

connection with Katrina since her participating in the class in 2011. She is on a journey of discovery and now is quite open to have discussions around who God is.

Approximately 40 percent of the Bible is narrative. There is an overarching story of God seeking to reconcile humanity to himself throughout the Bible. From the Old Testament introduction of God's reconciliation with Adam to the story of Jesus crucifixion and resurrection we see this narrative of reconciliation played out. What is consistently evident in Old Testament Scripture is that God's people, the Hebrew community, placed great importance on story, as did Jesus in his use of parable. N. T. Wright asserts that the vast majority of Scripture consists not in a list of rules or doctrines, but in narrative. The consistent story is God's desire to restore the world back to him and for his new kingdom to be set up in this world.[9]

Wright states that one of the key features of all worldviews is the element of story. This is of vital importance not least in relation to the New Testament and early Christianity, but this is in fact a symptom of a universal phenomenon. Story can help us in the first instance to articulate a critical-realist epistemology.[10] Often people in pain find it difficult to read or listen or hear directions or rules or regulations. But very frequently they are encouraged through story. Through the biblical metanarrative it is revealed that God desires not so much to judge humanity but to restore humanity. People usually react negatively when asked to change behavior. It causes a disconnect, but when their story is connected to the heart and purpose of God, the response changes. Once a person finds their place in that story they are able to connect others to the greater story of redemption. If a Christ-follower can invite an unchurched person to share their own individual story, it opens up an opportunity to bring a missional connection. This is a non-threatening, natural way to create an opportunity to bring Jesus into the conversation.

9. Wright, *New Testament and the People of God*, 32.
10. Ibid.

Jesus modeled a ministry of going out. Not only did he go from heaven to earth, he also went from temple to the world, not waiting for humanity to go to him. In the Gospel of Mark, Jesus spoke to people thirteen times by the lake, six times on the mountain, seven times in a house, twelve times in a town but only six times in the temple. Most of the church ministry is conducted in the church buildings. We conduct outreaches by inviting people to the church so that we can talk with them. Jesus commissioned the twelve and sent them out in pairs.[11] After the resurrection he appeared to Mary Magdalene at the tomb, he appeared to two of the disciples on the road to Emmaus, to the eleven while they were eating, but not once did he appear in the temple, and yet most of the current ministry is centered within the church buildings.

Jesus' fame spread as a storyteller. He engaged in parable and connected with the stories of individuals. A large percentage of the gospels are dedicated to narrative. When Peter spoke on the day of Pentecost, three thousand people were converted, he did not give them a list of rules, but retold their story and then connected their history with the saving grace of Jesus Christ. When Paul appeared before Agrippa he also recounted his story and connected his story to Jesus' saving grace. We need to actively look for ways that we can connect with the stories of those within our communities. We can no longer sit waiting for people in our neighborhoods to feel a need to attend a church to find God.

This book hopes to generate thoughts regarding opportunities to share the gospel with those who will not enter a church building. The focus will be on using art as that medium. It will look at the decline of the church in the Western world and the need to venture out into our communities with a message of love, grace, and reconciliation. It will cover the benefits of using art as that medium and document several art programs developed to make that connection. The hope is that the reader will identify ways in which art can be used to connect with those in their world and begin a journey of discovery of the Creator.

11. Mark 6.

1

The Decline of the Church
in the Western World

AUSTRALIA IS IN A post-Christian era. Recently I was invited to address the world religions class at a secular university. Over the previous weeks they had a Jewish rabbi, a Buddhist monk, a Muslim Imam and a Hindu visit to speak about their religion. Normally they invite a Catholic or Greek Orthodox priest to address the class, but this year someone had suggested me. So I was invited in to speak about my life as a female Christian minister.

Speaking at the university was confronting or challenging in many ways. It is the largest class in Melbourne of around 450 students, not all of them were there that day, but the session was recorded for the rest of the class. I spoke for an hour about my journey and the teachings of Jesus; this was followed by a time of questions and answers. The questions were not what I expected. I had read up on the atonement and different questions of deep theological significance. The priority for me was not to throw out trite answers to them.

But their questions were surprising. For example: How do you know that it is God speaking to you? If God is an interventionist why was there a holocaust? What is more important, to be in the church praying or to be helping in the community, as I was doing? Is Jesus a chauvinist? Why did he come as a man not a woman? These were the easy ones. Many of these are good, honest questions that people struggle with inside and outside of the church. The questions—and possibly some of the answers—would have been different twenty years ago, as our world is so different. I think it is really important that the church listen to these questions, rather than try to predict what we think the questions will be and supply our practiced responses.

The church in the Western world is in decline. In Australia approximately 90 percent of the population does not regularly attend a church.[1] Many of these have no understanding of the gospel message. America is heading the same way. Alvin Reid states that regular church attendance in America sits at 18 percent. He continues that more have a faith than attend a church.[2] Stanley Presser goes a step further, stating that at least 41 percent of Americans are hard-core unchurched. Most of these have no clear understanding of the gospel, and have had little or no contact with a Bible-teaching church.[3]

Ed Vitagliano writes, "Today Christianity is losing its light in the West but rising as the new light in Asia, Africa, and Latin America, West Africa, Latin America and Asia."[4] In the next fifty years, he assumes, those regions will become the new "spiritual home of faith." He adds that in 1900 there were approximately 10 million Christians in Africa; by 2000, the number had grown to 360 million.

However, the number of members within the Episcopal Church in the United States is declining, whereas in Uganda alone there are more than 8 million Anglicans. In terms of Evangelical Christians (the most thriving group), 70 percent of them live

1. NCLS Research, "National Church Life Survey 2011."

2. Reid, *Radically Unchurched*, cited at http://www.xenos.org/books/satan/churchdecline.htm.

3. Presser, "Data Collection Mode," 137–45.

4. Quoted in Park, "Scholars Find Decline of Christianity."

outside of the West.[5] David Barrett, coauthor of the *World Christian Encyclopedia*, reports that Africa is gaining 8.4 million new Christians a year.[6] South Korea grew from 300,000 in 1920 to 10 to 12 million, which is about 25 percent of the population.[7]

To add to the Western church problem, recent studies have shown that Evangelicals are not the fastest-growing faith group in America, neither are Pentecostals. The fastest-growing faith group in America is nonbelievers, in both numbers and percentages. From 1990 to 2001, they more than doubled, from 14 million to 29 million.[8]

Another startling figure is that out of all baptisms by Southern Baptists, only one in nine adults who were baptized described themselves as previously unchurched. In other words, eight of nine—almost 90 percent, of baptized adults had a connection with a church.[9] Reid continues, "Of the 350,000 churches in the United States, less than 1 percent is growing by conversion growth."[10] These statistics are more than frightening. We are going backwards, and it is essential that we look at how we are presenting the gospel.

Frequently, the strategy to reach those who do not have a Christian faith is an attractional model, which has limited success. In effect, the church is asking those outside of the faith to cross the missional road and attend a church. We are barely making an impact on the unchurched community. This book hopes to generate thoughts regarding opportunities to share the gospel with those who will not enter a church building.

Australian culture is different than it was thirty years ago, yet the church employs many of the same methods to reach people. The question that needs to be asked is why unchurched people would step into a church? Most of the unchurched would not

5. Ibid.
6. Ibid.
7. Ibid.
8. Quoted in McCallum, "Recent Research."
9. Reid, *Radically Unchurched*, cited at http://www.xenos.org/books/satan/churchdecline.htm.
10. Ibid.

consider visiting a church since they consider the church is for Christians, not for them. If the church is to impact community or make inroads into bridging the gap, we need to understand the culture and how ordinary Australians think and relate.

George Barna writes that attempting to get unchurched people to connect with God and his church solely by means of a worship service is shortsighted.[11] This form of evangelistic practice is unrealistic, and Christians need to discover how to relate to a postmodern worldview. This means being prepared to face a cross-cultural challenge.[12] The church in Australia is faced with a mission field within its own culture.[13] The missionary call is not to condemn or criticize culture, but rather to contextualize the good news into all cultures, even our own.[14] The end result is that it is imperative to know the culture we are relating to and develop the ability to relate the message in a way that it can be understood.

This conversation does not mean that the church needs to cease conducting the worship service, but it must consider the value of using the Sunday service as a means of evangelism. Only limited numbers of unchurched people will convert to Christianity in Australia and possibly America in this way. There are more effective ways to engage those outside of the church than inviting them to church services or events.

Gary Bouma, in his book *Australian Soul*, writes, "Religion in Australia is often treated with suspicion. From the early nineteenth century, religion in Australia was associated with a punitive imposed order. This was seen by many as an attempt to prohibit the few enjoyments open to an impoverished general population, and by others as an attempt to remove life-destroying evils of drinking, gambling and carousing."[15] To many Australians, the cultural view of religion is that it is designed to inhibit the enjoyment of life. This is sad.

11. Barna, *Grow Your Church*, 90.
12. Calver, "Postmodernism," 432.
13. Ibid.
14. Ibid., 433.
15. Bouma, *Australian Soul*, 11.

Bouma continues, "Australia has never been energetically religious like the USA, nor as secular as Sweden, but it is more of a place where religion and spirituality seem to be undergoing change rather than simple decline."[16] In postmodern Australia, there is an interest in spirituality, but it is distinct from religion. Religion is structured, communal and organizational; spirituality is personal, private and individualistic. Religion has negative connotations. Spirituality does not hold the same prejudice.[17]

Social researcher Mark McCrindle conducted a nationwide study on church attendance in Australia. He reports that "[people] like the product but they don't like the retail outlet . . . Even among those who identified themselves as religious, a quarter were not active at all in practising their faith and another 42 per cent rarely, if ever, worshipped as part of a group."[18] He continues, saying that church attendance in Australia has fallen to about one-in-thirteen people. That is between just 7 and 8 percent. These figures are extremely low.

Consider going to your mailbox to collect your mail and finding a brochure or an invitation inviting you to attend a Polish night. There would be Polish food, Polish conversation, Polish dancing, and Polish entertainment. Would you attend the Polish night? Most people probably would not attend because they are not Polish. And this is what often occurs when we put notices in our newspapers advertising our events and handing out our flyers, but unless someone has a connection they will not attend because they are not Christian. They believe that our great events and our wonderful advertising is about entertaining the Christians. This is rarely a form of evangelism that will reach the totally unchurched.

In the recent Australian census of 2011, the fastest growing group under the religious heading was those with no religion. So if only 7 percent of the Australian population regularly attend a church, there are some that are open to responding to an invitation to a church meeting. Let us try and put an estimated figure on this.

16. Ibid., 6.
17. Ibid., 15.
18. Quoted in Passmore, "We Believe."

I consider this percentage would be less than 13 percent. Let us be generous and say that 20 percent of our population would be open to respond to an invitation to a church meeting. Most churches spend most of their resources, time and finances targeting the 13 to 20 percent that may attend a church function, while there is little focus on the other 70 percent. This is where I believe that God has called me to respond. Sharing the gospel in this section takes a lot longer to get to, as we are starting much further back with the conversations.

7%	13–20%	70%
attending church	possibly open to visit if invited	would not think of attending a church

Jesus was very clear when he gave the command, in Mark 16:15, to "go into all the world and preach the good news."[19] It is limiting to stand on the inside of the church building and call to those on the outside to come in to them. The church must discover how to relate to people in the communities in which they exist. The Australian culture has changed, but the church in many cases has missed that change. We live in a postmodern, post-Christian world trying to relate the gospel with a modern message; this is like speaking Greek in Mexico. For many there is no connection with or understanding of the message. We need to be willing to face a cross-cultural challenge; to contextualize the gospel for those with whom it is being shared. We need to move outside of our confines and begin to create connection points with the people in the broader community.

Gary Bouma, in his book *Australian Soul*, writes that Australia is one of the most advanced multicultural societies on earth and has seen itself as a secular nation for decades.[20] Melbourne, with a population in excess of four million, is a city with people from

19. All Scripture quoted is from the New International Version unless otherwise noted.

20. Bouma, *Australian Soul*, 3.

all walks of life.[21] It is home to many Muslims and Christians, but most Melbournians do not have much of a religious conviction.

Although Australia has an excellent welfare system by world standards, the reality is that on a daily basis people struggle to meet their house repayments or to pay rent. Ten years ago it seemed many families had a choice about having one parent stay at home to raise the family, whereas today this can no longer be taken for granted. This pressure is real, with many couples considering whether they can afford a family or purchase a home.[22] With the global economic situation this is a growing trend.

There is a perception of what provisions are necessary for a family to bring up a healthy, well-adjusted child. This includes the need to provide for an education, as well as extracurricular activities. The pressure for this is very real.[23] Australia is referred to as a sporting nation, with sport in Australia being more than just a pastime. It plays a major role in shaping the country's identity and culture, so much so that sport is often referred to as "Australia's national religion."[24]

Due to this, there is a sense that most children should be involved in at least one sport. Almost 70 percent of Australians aged fifteen years and over participate at least once a week in physical activity for exercise, recreation and sport.[25] With several children in a family that may mean the family is involved in several sporting events. With limited networks and family support, the income required to sustain the level of commitment to get to these events, ferrying children on game day, attending practices, the cost of the training, uniforms and sporting fees is enormous. It is a strain on the family unit. Then there are the other activities, such as music, art and other outside leisure activities. This in turn has an overflow into relationships, and this is added pressure in life.

21. Australian Bureau of Statistics, "Year Book Australia, 2004."

22. Flynn, "Home Ownership Dream Fading."

23. Australian Bureau of Statistics, "Year Book Australia, 2004."

24. Australian Dept. of Foreign Affairs, "Sport Performance and Participation."

25. Ibid.

The Orygen Research Centre has conducted studies on the mental health of Australians. Their statistics show that in one year, almost 20 percent of adults suffer from common mental disorders.[26] "A mental disorder is a diagnosable illness which causes major changes in a person's thinking, emotional state and behavior, and disrupts the person's ability to study or work and carry on their usual personal relationships."[27] In this case, the disorders referred to are often depression or anxiety.

The Department of Health suggests that "anxiety disorders are the most common form of mental illness, and affect one in twenty people at any given time."[28] Anxiety disorders affect the way a person thinks, feels and behaves and, if not treated, can cause considerable distress and disruption to the person's life. Add to this those who may not themselves be suffering a mental illness but are impacted by it through relationships with family, relatives, friends and colleagues. The consequence is a community that is affected and hindered in everyday life and interactions. The result is a community whose relationships, working life and social interactions are diminished because of the torment of mental illness.

On consultation with the local community health center, it became evident there are many young women that visit the maternal community health centers in my local community struggling with postnatal depression.[29] The maternal health nurse suggested there are two fairly defined groups of women visiting the health centers. First, the women who usually work, and are often quite aware of their depression and reasonably motivated to do something about it.

However, there is another group: Many of these women have moved into this area due to more affordable housing, but left their families and support networks. In many instances their partners leave home early to commute to work and return late in the

26. Quoted in Kitchener and Jorm, *Youth Mental Health*, 11.

27. Andrews et al., *Mental Health of Australians*, 11.

28. Australian Dept. of Health, "What Is an Anxiety Disorder?," 2.

29. Interview with Sue Weston, community health nurse, Beaconsfield community health center, 15 June 2011.

evening, leaving the women isolated and alone at home with their babies. These long days reinforce their experience of depression. We need to understand their lifestyle, their worldview and their questions. We need to get out of our confines and begin conversations with our communities.

It is essential for us to know our communities. To understand what is happening outside of our churches and to be able to contextualize the gospel to those who hear it. We need to be able to objectively look at what is working. See what things the people around us are facing and connect with them through whatever means, to be able to share the grace and mercy that we ourselves have discovered.

2

How on Earth Should
the Church Operate?

I LOVE READING JESUS' story; it's so unexpected. We develop a picture or a vision of what he is like and how he was when he walked the earth. But frequently it is just so different than the Jesus we see in Scripture. I appreciate that he did the opposite than what was expected. I enjoy reading of his teachings and his interactions. I love that he put himself out there for the unlovely and unimportant. He risked isolation, segregation and seclusion for the sake of others. He faced being cut off from his people. Jesus became ceremonially unclean to sit with the leper, the prostitute, and the adulterer, the Samaritan, the Syro-Phoenecian. He gained the scorn of the popular to dine with the tax collector. This is a wonderful, frightening, challenging story that unfolds on the pages of the Bible. This causes me to question: Is this what he expects of me?

Many do not know how to relate to those outside of the church. Recently we were organizing to run an Art for Justice stall at the local market.[1] I received a Facebook message from a lady saying that her husband was holding a stall there handing out Christian tracts. This may have worked some time ago, but

---

1. This is recorded in chapter 6.

rarely in a post-Christian era. Often we have groups of people that want to join us at Art and Soul, and I love this, but at times their ideas and what we are doing do not match up. We had a couple of musicians come to play with us one Sunday morning. Their pastor turned up around noon, once their church service had finished, to see what they were doing. He began to ask about Art for Justice and how it ran. His response was that they might do this, too. They could set up a prayer tent and put literature out. This would be great for those who are seeking and open, but we have discovered that most of the market goers are far from this point. They do not have an interest in reading literature and are often suspicious of prayer, particularly in a prayer tent. Some will respond, but the majority are not interested in listening to a conversation on Christianity from people that they do not know.

The intent of the church should be to bring hope and life to a hurt and broken world (see Luke 4:18), but so often the attention and resourcing is focused on maintaining itself. Often those that the church is called to reach with love and grace have little understanding of who the church is. In Matthew 9:12, Jesus reveals he came for those who do not know him. I think we often get it the wrong way around. We expend so much energy and so many resources on propping up the inner workings—programs, events, keeping people happy, providing the desires of those who are inside the four walls. Not that this is wrong, but when the majority of the focus remains in here, and there is so much adventure to be had connecting with the community outside the church, it seems a little sad.

James Thwaites, writes that the church has located the Son of God in a far-removed, indefinable, and transcendent heaven that has little to do with this age and most to do with an afterlife.[2] For the unchurched, God seems remote, often disapproving. Going to church at times may be a little like going to visit an elderly grandfather in an aged care facility. We go to church to connect with God, whereas he is so at work outside in the community. Yes, even with those who do not know him, he is active.

2. Thwaites, *Church beyond the Congregation*, 5.

Over the last few years I developed several initiatives to connect with the broader community and generate missional conversations through the medium of art. This is not just art for art's sake but with a definitive purpose of engaging with the people that would not enter a church. These initiatives are tools for connection designed to open up conversation points. These conversations often lead to an ongoing journey and continuing dialogue. Some of these may lead to a person finding relationship with Jesus. For some it may purely be to create a place for a question of God to be formed.[3]

Many have commenced a journey that connects with other art initiatives within the Kaleidoscope community. These initiatives may include Patmos Artist Network, those attending the "at-risk" teen group may go from Art and Soul to Art for Justice or vice versa.[4] Either way the ongoing journey encourages continued conversations. Some do not go any further than an initial conversation, but something can still be imparted that plants a seed that others may have the benefit of adding to. As Paul writes, "I planted the seed, Apollos watered it, but God has been making it grow."[5] At the very least, a love or interest in art may have been established.

In church life, we get so caught up trying to get people to attend our events. A friend who has been in ministry for years was visiting recently from interstate. He told me that they expected that their church would have grown when they moved from a rental premises into their own building. When I asked why he thought it would grow, he responded that they had bought chairs for the new building, they had prayed over them and believed that God would fill them. The conversation went on to the fact of real frustration with the people at church because they did not invite their friends, they did not bring them along to events or special church services. I asked whether he and his wife modeled that. Did they

3. Refer to graph in chapter 1.

4. Patmos Artist Network is an artists' network overseen by Kaleidoscope that encourages emerging artists, runs art classes and encourages artist community. See http://patmos.webs.com.

5. 1 Cor 3:6.

bring people along? There was no answer. Often we think that the unchurched will wake up one day and realize their lack of spiritual fulfillment and then know that they need to go to a church to fill that void. This rarely happens.

Church life consumes the time, thoughts, activities and resources of its members often to the detriment of their families and lives outside of the building. When we moved to the house we live in now, we had been in ministry for many, many years and we were tired. I remember saying to Mick (my husband), "When did we stop having people in our home?" I do not know when it happened. We had always had people coming in and out of our home, but I realized that at some point we had stopped inviting people over so frequently. Church life had consumed us. We had meetings most nights of the week and when we didn't we were too tired to connect meaningfully. As we moved to our new house, I went out and bought a twelve-seat table. It was a statement. We were going to fling our doors open and start connecting again.

Bill Dyrness, in his book *Senses of the Soul*, writes, "In many instances the Great Commission has been watered down to a measurable objective and converted into maximizing numbers of converts to church members, it has diminished Christ's command to make disciples in all nations. When the aim is at what can be measured the most important goals of character, discipleship and holiness are ignored, which cannot be predicted or quantified without falling into legalism."[6] When a value cannot be measured, value is placed instead on what can be measured. This may end up being more about quantity than quality at times. Because of this, the focus needs to shift from attempting to build the church, which was never our imperative. Building the church is Jesus' role, we need to shift our focus to making disciples. This begins by each Christ follower connecting and conversing with the people that their lives intersect with on a daily basis.

Reggie McNeal, in his book *Missional Renaissance*, writes about changing the scorecard of what is measured in churches.[7]

6. Dyrness, *Senses of the Soul*, 88.
7. McNeal, *Missional Renaissance*.

Art and Soul

Numerical growth as a strategic goal has no scriptural foundation whatsoever. When it is a driving focus, there is a strong tendency to base programs on those activities that attract the most newcomers and produce the greatest retention among existing members. Dyrness states that these numbers are all too often attracted by skillful marketing methods, thus supplanting the slow work of Christian nurturing.[8] He makes the observation that often there are large meetings with tens or hundreds of people making commitments to follow Jesus but questions whether this is effective in the long term. He writes, "The reign of Christ and his kingdom is extended one light at a time. Hundreds are often converted through mass evangelism but often there is very little light in spite of the numbers."[9]

After being impacted by McNeal's book, we decided to work on what we were measuring at Kaleidoscope.[10] We had a couple of nights dedicated to looking at our scorecard. As we discussed it, I said to the team, "I am not sure what we need to measure but I am clear on what won't be a measurement. We won't measure bums on seats and money in the offering." One of our team, Paul, quickly responded, "Well maybe instead of that, we could measure how many seats we offer, and how much money we give the bums." I like that measure so much more.

We need to be concerned with movement of people from church buildings into the community. It is important to recognize there seems to exist a cultural divide between the church and the community that needs to be crossed. Missionaries have successfully bridged this divide for centuries. Their contributions and practices may inform the methodology of going out into the community.

Paul Fiddes makes the point that the gospel story of salvation is of a "sending" mission: the Father sends out the Son into the world, into ministry in Galilee, into the conflict of Jerusalem, and on resurrection morning out into Galilee again, into the land

8. Dyrness, *Senses of the Soul*, 114.
9. Ibid., 83.
10. Kaleidoscope is an alternative style church that I planted in 2010.

14

bordering the lands of the Gentiles. After this the Son sends out the Spirit from his Father into the life of his disciples, and they in turn are sent with the ministry of reconciliation beyond the borders of Galilee into the whole world. This story of sending at a particular time and place in history has its roots in an eternal sending within God. The two missions in the world, of the Word and the Spirit, were based in two "processions" in the inner being of God.[11] Yet most effort and resource are spent on getting people into the church building rather than following *missio Dei*. Leonard Sweet adds, "Jesus said, 'Go make disciples,' we stopped and built worship warehouses."[12]

The reality is Jesus met with people out in the communities, the temple courtyard, in the town, in houses and the countryside. Ministry was not confined to the synagogue. In the same way, church is not the only place where ministry occurs. Too frequently Christians go to church to encounter God, but God is out in the community. Jesus meets with people while they are walking and eating and living life. He is involved in the everyday lives of people.

Jesus spent most of his time and ministry outside of the temple. As spoken of in chapter 1, we see his ministry was by the lake, on the mountain, in a house, in a town, but only six times in the temple. After the resurrection we do not read about him ministering in the temple, yet our ministry is consistently focused within church buildings.

God does not look for the expert to deliver the good news. The first person that Jesus chose to share the good news of the resurrection with was not the most respected, or articulate or theologically trained; added to that, it was a woman, and not only a woman, but one of ill repute, and she was demon possessed (Mark 16:9). Jesus uses the ordinary, the everyday person to carry his transforming power to his world. The qualification for this according to 2 Corinthians 5:17 is anyone in Christ. Many came to faith and followed Christ. The focus needs to be upon every believer going and sharing their story, rather than inviting people to church

11. Fiddes, *Participating in God*, 7.

12. Sweet, *I Am a Follower*, 70.

to hear the message. Romans 10:8 poses the question, how will those who have not heard believe?

Over the years what has occurred is that the Sunday morning service has become the major evangelistic tool of the church. This is added to a few strategically placed events or meetings designed to attract the unchurched. This style of evangelism prevents the building of relationship or community. Grenz notes that members of the next generation are often unimpressed by verbal presentations of the gospel. What they want to see are a people who live out the gospel in wholesome, authentic and healing relationships.[13] Although these meetings may be articulate and polished, the question that needs to be asked is whether they are effective.

In Acts 1, Jesus promised the Holy Spirit would come to empower his followers and empower them to be witnesses. These are the followers of Jesus. In Acts 2, on the day of Pentecost, the Holy Spirit descended upon the disciples and empowered them for ministry. From here they went out into their communities sharing the good news. They opened their homes and gathered together sharing meals and stories.

In Acts 8, just prior to Stephen's martyrdom, great persecution broke out against the church and all except the apostles were scattered. The word scatter (*diaspeiro*), means to scatter abroad, but it also means to sow seed.[14] This Scripture can be interpreted to mean that those who were scattered were actually sown. They left where they were and were sown into the world around them; this resulted in major church growth with an influx of believers. We need to see ourselves as sown into community rather than inviting people to church meetings.

I was a hippie in Tasmania when I became a follower of Christ. This encounter changed my life totally. I led many people into a discovery of relationship with God over the first few years. My husband and I moved to a commune and shared our story there. Twelve of the hippies became Christ followers. We were not trained in evangelism or ministry. In fact we were only one step

13. Grenz, *Theology for the Community of God*, 169.

14. *Vine's Complete Expository Dictionary*, s.v. "diaspeiro."

ahead of them. They would ask a question and we would respond by telling them that we would discuss that question tomorrow and we would feverishly search the Scriptures for a response.

Somewhere along the way this ceased, or at least diminished. We realized that the place for Christians was in the church, and ministry became about looking after those in the church. This is a very valid ministry. But if we all start doing this, we are shrinking the powerful force that we are intended to be.

We have seen this pattern in the church over the centuries. It began well. But in AD 313 Constantine declared that Christianity would be the religion of the empire. It went from margins to mainstream and everything changed. It became the state religion and did not change for centuries. During the Dark Ages there was not much light in the church, and we see it descend into a very transactional style faith—if I behave this way, or pay tithes, or work hard then I will find favor. The sixteenth-century Reformation, when Luther nailed the ninety-five theses on the Castle Church door on October 31, 1517, split the Western church into Roman Catholic and Protestant. At this point there was a shift in Christianity and a resurgence in the church. Again the church spread.

Alan and Debra Hirsch state that when we look at the early church we are confronted with the reality of a people movement where everyone is regarded as a significant agent of the King and is encouraged to find their place in the unfolding of the movement.[15] Every person, regardless of whether they are a new convert or a mature believer, is invited to be involved in extending the kingdom of God. Although it is often unstructured and messy, the invitation is for all to belong and to participate.

It is essential to teach people in the community to connect with their families, friends, neighbors, workmates and encourage them to engage in missional conversations. It takes a deliberate decision to move outside of the church building and into the community. At times it seems almost like a magnet drawing all the attention back to the inside.

15. Hirsch and Hirsch, *Untamed*, 142.

Art and Soul

It does not need to be over complicated. A couple of months after moving into our neighborhood we held a street party. It was approaching Christmas, so I simply walked around and deposited an invitation into the letterboxes of the people on our street. We provided meat and asked them to bring either a salad or dessert and bring their own drinks. We dragged our barbeque and a table into our driveway. Every single one of our neighbors came. It has changed how we relate to one another. It was a very easy way to connect. We continue the tradition each year.

Too often we want to get to the end of the conversation before we have started. I do not need to spell out a three-step plan of salvation on a first meeting. I do not need to tell them I'm a Christian when I first get to know them. I do not need to invite them to church in the first week of meeting them.

So how do we go into a biblically illiterate culture with a gospel message? Art is an easy access. It can be confrontational without confronting. Art in its pure form is inoffensive. This strategy is not one of people looking at art alone, it is one of engagement. The point is to invite people to participate rather than spectate by connecting people with their creative side. This in turn may cause a questioning to begin within the hearts and minds of the people who are involved.

Craig Detweiler's book *Purple State of Mind* speaks of how culture has been divided spiritually, politically and morally into really defined segments. He refers to these as red and blue states. His thesis states that the Christian message has often been drowned out to the hearers by the harsh propagation of the message. He writes that Christians need a different kind of apologetic.[16] He refers to this apologetic as the "purple state." The purple state is not a compromised position, but one that listens to the words and questions of others and responds meekly with grace. This posture begins from a position of humility rather than pronouncement.

Detweiler poses the question, "How do we remove the barrier that we have erected through our polarizing and politicized faith?" He continues that it is important to find common ground

16. Detweiler, *Purple State of Mind*, 10.

18

rather than bones of contention.[17] Removing barriers is more about beginning a conversation than starting an argument. Too often, Christians have become famous for what they oppose rather than what they stand for. People often state they would not be welcome in church as their lifestyles would not be conducive to church life. The reality is that many of the issues these individuals have are not on the list of importance in following Jesus.

Detwieler writes, "Artists are comfortable living on the margins, challenging notions such as 'comfort equals happiness.' They also understand the power of observation, of stillness, of learning to see God in nature and everyday life. A visual faith can simplify our levels and deepen our discipleship."[18] This quote provides insight into why artists are ready to push beyond the point of what is known into unknown. He continues that great art begins with enduring questions.[19] He also suggests that imagination is an act of faith, an ability to see a world of possibilities despite distractions and destructions.[20] Art is an easy way to cross many barriers.

17. Ibid., 16.
18. Ibid., 92.
19. Ibid., 97.
20. Ibid., 99.

3

God, Art, and Creativity

ART HAS ALWAYS BEEN used to tell God's story. From the beginning of time we see art and creativity presented in the pages of the Bible. I do not think that most people realize how big an impact that art can have in revealing God. I remember trying to explain my final project at Fuller. I knew I wanted to write my project on the missional use of art to connect with people. When I first began speaking to my project adviser, he understood that I was doing something around art and evangelism. But he, like most people that I spoke to, thought that the plan would be that I would paint a painting and someone would come along and be overcome and say, "Wow there must be a God." It took me an hour on a Skype conversation to explain that it was not about me painting for others to see, but that it was about engaging with others through the process and experience of art. It's such a powerful place to be involved, to see people shift from left brain to right brain: from the logical side to a more creative space.[1]

Art is a powerful medium. Something within the heart of humanity and the creative essence calls to a place within the heart. There is a sense of satisfaction after being involved creatively.

1. See Hicks, "Who Stole the Right Side of Your Brain?"

Creativity often begins with a question. John Paul II states, "Art asks questions concerning the hidden meaning of things and ultimately the very meaning of human existence."[2] It not only connects with the creativity in humanity, it opens up a dialogue or forms a question. To limit art as either a secular or Christian pursuit diminishes the capacity or possibility of Creator God to use this to touch a hurt and broken world.

God is the originator of creativity. The earth, God's masterpiece, reveals creativity in every aspect. Psalm 19 speaks of the natural revelation of God: His revelation of himself to humanity through his creation. The world itself, by the fact that it exists, testifies to the Creator. The language in the first two verses of this psalm—"declare," "proclaim," "pour forth," "displays"—attests to the fact that God, through his creation, desires for humanity to know him. The world itself is viewed as a creative text authored by God, of which humanity, as interpreters, are an integral part.

God intended his creation to be both functional and beautiful (Gen 2:9). The climax of his creative power was humanity, made in his image and likeness, the *imago Dei*, humanity unique among God's creatures, all worthy of honor and respect. By the fact that they exist and are in his image, they have incredible value and worth. God's nature and divine creativity are intrinsically woven into the essence of creation. Pure functionality is only half the picture. A work of art has value as a creation because human beings are made in the image of God, and have the capacity to create.

Martin Luther wrote that God, the Creator, invited Adam to share in the process of creation. He permitted humans to take the elements of his cosmos and create new arrangements with them. This may explain the reason why creating anything is so fulfilling.[3] There is a desire to express creatively. That may outwork itself in different ways: cooking, gardening, mechanics, building, inventing, sewing, or many other creative forms. There is something inherent within humanity to desire to create or form. It is a God-given gift. Art is such a powerful tool on so many levels. Humanity

2. As quoted in Freddoso, "Church and Art."
3. Luther, "Open Letter."

was created not just to appreciate the creative expression, but also to be to be involved in it.

We hold a creative worship night at Kaleidoscope about once every two months. This night is about exploring different forms of worship. I believe that generally in the church we have become fairly set in how we conduct worship and how we engage. The creative worship nights commence with the sharing of a passage of Scripture, spending about twenty minutes focusing and teaching on the passage. From here people choose to be part of different groups. For example, song writing—those in the song-writing groups write a song on the shared scriptural passage. Another group will paint the passage. A third group engages with collage, where they use mixed mediums to create some art form on a canvas that encompasses the same theme. Another group takes part in a deeper discussion of the Scripture and how that outworks in life today. The final group creatively writes on the topic. Amazing poems have been produced on this night. I am currently working on adding in a new group that will cook. Many people tell me that they feel close to God when they cook for others. So we will add a cooking group to the next creative worship night. I am not sure how they will cook the theme of the night, but we will work on something.

After an hour or so participating in these groups, everyone comes together to go a little deeper with the teaching. They then return to their groups to complete their work. About an hour later everyone comes together, and each group shares their thoughts, songs, paintings, and writings. It is a really powerful time in which people can form and express different styles of creativity and explore ways of connecting to God and to one another.

Creativity is inherent. The Hebrew word *bara*, which is used for describing God's creation work in Genesis 1 and 2, means "to create, shape, form, make."[4] The verb expresses creation out of nothing.[5] Other verbs for creating allow a broader range of meaning. This is possibly best expressed in Isaiah 45:18: "For thus

4. *Strong's Exhaustive Concordance*, H1254.

5. *Vine's Complete Expository Dictionary*, s.v. "bara."

saith the Lord that created [*bara*] the heavens; God himself that formed [*yasar*—'to form'] the earth and made [*asah*—'to make, to assemble together with existing materials'] it; he has established [*kun*—'to establish'] it, he created [*bara*] it not in vain, he formed [*yasar*] it to be inhabited: I am the Lord; and there is nothing else." In this text, along with *bara* the verb *yasar* occurs twice. Walter Brueggemann asserts that this verb reflects the imagery of a potter forming clay, thus working an existing material. The term has connotations of active, material engagement with the stuff of creation, in an artistic endeavor.[6]

Julia Cameron, in her book *The Artist's Way*, writes that all have inherent creativity, but to really connect with that creativity one needs to connect with the Creator. It takes a step of faith to make that connection and release the creativity within. "For most of us, the idea that the creator encourages creativity is a radical thought."[7] Her book gives people a place to begin in releasing creativity while explaining the purposes behind it.

Even after the fall, once we see the entrance of sin and brokenness, this creativity remained. Humanity is both an image-bearer and morally crippled. Works of art are therefore bittersweet. John Calvin acknowledged this tension when he said, "The human mind, however much fallen and perverted from its original integrity, is still adorned and invested with admirable gifts from its Creator. Humanity can produce art, which reflects the Creator, but also the "fallen-ness" of humanity and anything in between.[8] We see the evidence of broken beauty, which reveals the complexity of the human experience.

But not only are we able to create in our brokenness, it may be seen as a commissioned calling by the Father. The biblical account of Jubal, "the first of all who play the harp and flute," and also of Tubal Cain, who forged tools out of bronze and iron, is found in Genesis 4:21. Right at the beginnings of human existence, humanity began to put into practice the God-given creative gifts.

6. Brueggemann, *Theology of the Old Testament*, 147.
7. Cameron, *Artist's Way*, 17.
8. Calvin, *Institutes*, 236.

Throughout the Bible, God encourages, even commissions artists to produce works that reveal him or his purposes. In Exodus 35:30 it says, "See, I have chosen Bezalel son of Uri, the son of Hur, of the tribe of Judah." The word *qara*, translated "chosen" in this verse, is a word that means "called or commissioned."[9] Vines speak of it as the specification of a naming.[10] This has the same connotations as God calling light day and darkness night. The same creative force is utilized as God's act of creating and naming stars. This calling relates to a specific task. God commissions Bezalel son of Uri for the work of overseeing the building of the tabernacle. He is releasing that same creative *qara* in the implementation of his calling or commissioning.

Bezalel was a master craftsman. He had a specific call to make "artistic designs." This opens up the possibility of artistic expression as a spiritual calling. He was filled with the Spirit of God in knowledge, skill and ability to do the work of building the tabernacle. The Old Testament is rich with examples, which confirm the artistic dimension. There is incredibly intricate artistic design in the building of the tabernacle and eventually the temple, conceived and designed by God, then related to and executed by his human artisans and builders.[11] In Numbers 21:4–9, God directs Moses to make a sculpture of a snake, this was a visual representation as a means to bring forgiveness, healing and restoration to his people. Although the Old Testament forbids the making of "graven images" used in idolatry, it uses art and craftsmanship in the act of worship to God.

Harbinson writes, "Before the arts can take their God-ordained place within the church and in the culture at large, there must be a recovery of a biblical understanding of the arts to the glory of God that ignites the imagination. When this happens, the calling of the artist will be affirmed, recognized and supported."[12] I believe that there is a new appreciation for art within the church.

9. *Strong's Exhaustive Concordance*, 105.

10. *Vine's Complete Expository Dictionary*, s.v. "qara."

11. Luther, "Open Letter."

12. Harbinson, "Restoring the Arts."

The church is reclaiming art and we are seeing art pastors, artists painting sermons, installing art shows and so many more expressions of art and creativity.

DeConcini writes that prior to 1500, the church was dominated by ideas that holy callings to be a priest, a monk or a nun were somehow the only way to really please God. Art, or secular work, was not a calling. However, art and spirituality can work hand-in-hand. The two can nourish one another. Shaw writes that they work in tandem; it is hard to imagine an artist who is totally unspiritual in the sense of being out of touch with both created and unseen worlds.[13] Because of the separation of art from faith, an important vehicle of the creative expression has been cut off.

The church is divided on the subject of art. There are great extremes, from the luxuriant artistic expression found within Catholic and Anglican cathedrals to the absence of artistic expression on the walls of the Amish homesteads. The Amish *Ordnung* expresses that art for art's sake is considered worldly and wasteful.[14] Artistic expression needs to have a functional value, instead of strictly aesthetic purposes.

The Christian church itself uses symbols of the cross and fish. There is a plethora of symbolism and story in stained glass, painting and sculpture within church buildings. Some of the greatest works in history have been of religious origin. Michelangelo is famous for his paintings in the Sistine Chapel and his sculpture of David, as is Da Vinci for his portrayal of the Last Supper. Many artists have told and retold the story of Jesus over the centuries.

Christian art has been seen as iconic symbolism for inside the church. However, art is broader than that. Mennekes writes, "I would say art is not needed in a church, we do not need any art. But we need all art. So then art is needed, but not Christian subjects in art."[15] It is not that Christian art is wrong or unneeded, but broader and deeper than that. Art connects with the spiritual

---

13. Shaw, "Art and Christian Spirituality," 36.
14. The Amish *Ordnung* is an Amish set of rules to live by.
15. Mennekes, "Art of Spirituality."

without the cross and the fish. It belongs to humanity and is able
to reveal the Creator to the creation.

There is not a lot to be found historically in regard to painting
within the church meeting until the last fifteen years or so. There
has been a recent emergence of art creeping into Sunday services
over the last few years. At Kaleidoscope each week we have at
least two artists painting the message. It gives a different picture
to the message than only a word sermon. This is becoming more
common in churches, with painting being used in a prophetic
sense in worship.

I recall the first time I painted in church. It was Pentecost Sunday. Jenny was painting with me. We set our easels up at the front
of the church, hers on the right and mine on the left. Jenny began
to paint several beautiful clay pots with oil spilling over the sides.
She was representing the oil of the Holy Spirit being poured out. I
had decided to paint the tongues of fire appearing on the heads of
the people on the day of Pentecost. I should have taken more time
to think about it. As usual, I bit off a little more than I could chew.
It would have been fine if I had painted one person, but I decided to
paint three.

About half way through the painting I realized this was a big
task, possibly bigger than I had time for. I took a couple of steps back
from the easel to have a look at my work and as I looked, I was hor-
rified. The tongues of fire looked like flames, which were good, but
it actually looked like I was painting the disciples burning in hell. I
quickly tried to paint smiles on their faces, which started to look like
they were grimacing. I looked around this large church; everyone
was watching my work as they listened to the sermon. I decided I
just had to forget those looking on and try to create something. I put
my head down and painted and painted and finally something appeared that was passable. My biggest lesson this day was to simplify
the work. I cannot paint a masterpiece in little more than an hour. In
this context I am painting a message. Simple is beautiful.

Creativity is intrinsic to humanity. Every culture in the
world produces art. There is no society that does not attempt to
decorate its surroundings, clothing or the body, or to represent

its cultural, historic story in art. The Australian Aborigine is one of the most ancient cultures. Aboriginal people have long artistic traditions within which they use common designs and symbols. These designs have the power to transform the object to one with religious significance and power.[16] They use a term, "The Dreaming," to describe the balance between the spiritual, natural and moral elements of the world. It relates to a period from the origin of the universe, a time of creator ancestors and supernatural beings who formed the features of the land and all living things and also set down the laws for social and moral order. The Dreaming, as well as answering questions about origins, provides a framework for human experience in the universe and the place of all living things within it.[17]

Art brings richness to a culture. Louise Johnson writes that where creativity has been fostered there is a marked change to the environment. Blighted urban environments are regenerated, populations enlivened and economies boosted through the mobilization of the arts. The intentional theme of this has spread across the world since the mid-1980s.[18] Graeme Evans concurs, "Today, when cities or regional communities confront the loss of population or employment and consider how to become more attractive to investors and tourists, a commonly pursued policy is to actively grow the arts."[19] The creative arts are seen as a way to both culturally enrich local populations and to offer them economic salvation. If this is true for the general population, how much more for the church, the people of God. Intentionally valuing and introducing the arts help create a better world to live in.

Christianity in Australia in the early convict days was extremely harsh. Some artists who were transported to Australia were required to use their artistic skills as servants. Others were not permitted to practice their art until they had received pardons from their sentences. The common theme was that artists

16. See "Dreaming and the Dreamtime," AboriginalArtOnline.com.
17. Ibid.
18. Johnson, "Valuing Arts," 471.
19. Evans, "Measure for Measure," 983.

used their art to record and interpret the landscape and people of the fledgling colony. Their artwork contributed enormously to the understanding of early nineteenth-century Australia.[20] Art captured and told the story of people from all walks of life in these pioneering days.

As we have seen, people seek to make sense of life and their environment. From the oldest cultures, stories can be read, from cave drawings to hieroglyphics. These cultural stories are related through art. In almost every culture there has also been a close tie between religion and art. It speaks of their belief and worldview. Religion seeks answers to those "most vital personal questions" that art in its own way wishes to address: questions concerning the very meaning of human existence.[21] There are common questions within the heart of humanity: Who am I and what am I here for? People seek an answer to these questions. These same questions are asked and attempts made to answer in the field of art also.

Jean Baudrillard writes that art should be an affirmation of life, not an attempt to bring order, but simply a way of waking up to the very life we are living.[22] Art invites the question, it has the capacity to begin the conversation, to connect with the Creator. It attempts to make sense of life. It may not positively answer the questions, but perhaps it can cause the conversation to begin.

Art often speaks subliminally, or subconsciously, beyond awareness. This kind of information supersedes cognitive reasoning. In that regard, art—poetry, music, painting, dance—assists the onlooker to gain insight, to see beyond what can be seen with the eye; it has the ability to open up a curiosity within. Even those who have not connected with their creativity can have an appreciation of what is made or created. Sayers wrote, "The words of creeds come before our eyes and ears as pictures."[23] The mind takes the words and an image forms. God consistently uses stories

20. See "Convict Artists in Governor Macquarie's Era," State Library of New South Wales.
21. Freddoso, "Church and Art."
22. Baudrillard, *Revenge of the Crystal*, 63.
23. Sayers, "Mind of the Maker," 20.

to create images by which people learn; there is no need to explain imagery. The learning happens unconsciously and often a spiritual connection is made.

The process of creating art can itself be a pathway of discovery, a way of discovering meaning and purpose. Christians never fully arrive, but deeper truths are revealed as they explore. Spirituality is an encounter with the mystery of relationship with God. By creating art there are often stirrings and insights discovered through the process of creativity, which leads to discovery of God, or at least a hunger for meaning.

Psychologist Viktor Frankl developed a school of therapy after being in a concentration camp and discovering that those who were able to create a sense of meaningfulness fared much better than those who did not. He described the search for meaning in one's life as "the primary motivational force" in people.[24] Spirituality and meaning can be cultivated through art. If those the church tries to communicate with do not listen, there is little point in speaking. Art-making goes beyond entertainment and self-expression. To make and enjoy art seems to be universal, whether in the form of painting, music or poetry. It can open up the world we live in, and in unique ways, becoming a vehicle of discovery.

It is essential that God's story is told in a way that people in the community can understand. Christian concepts are often foreign to them. But if the church can interpret the heart of God for an individual or a group of people and paint it in language they can understand there is an opportunity for a missional conversation to begin. An effective medium to both relate and receive an individual's deeper story is through art. Art can be deeply spiritual in that it delves below the surface and asks questions.

There is inspiration at the foundation of every work of art. The artist's revelation is placed upon a canvas and the spectator is invited to engage. These two arenas of art and spirituality collide, which enables the artist to function as both an artisan and a storyteller, allowing spirituality to be revealed through the creation. The purpose of the art is to create a response.

24. Frankl, *Man's Search for Meaning*, 153.

4

Art as an Integral Expression of Mission

A FEW YEARS AGO I went through what I call the dark period; although I can be a little dramatic, this was a really low time in my life. I found myself in a very difficult situation at work. I had been in ministry for many years. I was associate minister, second in charge of a large church, and work and ministry became extremely difficult. I was cut off from my friendships that had been established over many years. I was isolated from anyone that I may have processed these things with. And in the midst of this, it was almost like God went silent. All the normal connection places that I was familiar with and had established over the years were seemingly silent and barren.

In the midst of this, I began to listen to worship music and then began to paint. I painted and painted and painted.[1] I painted my way through this period and in the midst of it I found God, not the answer to my questions. But I discovered God in a totally different way than I had ever known him before. It changed my life.

During this time several people tried to give me trite answers, which made my pain greater. I felt like a bad Christian, let alone

1. See my website, www.michellesanders.com.au.

minister, as I grappled with issues in my life. During this, my biggest struggle was a desire to be authentic while in the midst of this storm. This lasted several years.

The psalms give us a place to voice our disappointment our struggles and our doubts, our triumphs. We see the writers give voice and resolve, maybe not resolve, but come to a place of faith and acceptance of the mystery of their journey. The book of Psalms gives us a wonderful place to be able to gain strength and understanding. The pages of our ancient writings hold the wisdom of the ages.

The Bible is a literary painting. It is one of the most spectacular literary pieces of all time. Henry Halley refers to Genesis 1:1—2:3 as the "Creation Hymn" and describes it as poetic verse in measured, majestic movement, containing the successive steps of creation, cast in the mold of the recurring biblical "seven."[2] It is only fitting that this account should be one of creativity in every form. Brueggemann states that this account does not particularly invite speculation or explanation. It invites wonder, awe.[3]

The writings reveal God himself, the meaning of what humanity is here for; it tells the story of redemption and gives revelation. Martin Luther writes that the entire Bible is not only revelation; it is itself a work of art. And this work of art "has been the single greatest influence on art."[4]

As the Bible unfolds, it does so in stories and poetry. Approximately 40 percent of Scripture consists of narrative. Fifteen percent is expressed in poetic form, and only 10 percent is propositional and overtly instructional in nature.[5] The Bible is filled with symbolism and imagery. According to Luther, "It sheds more light upon the creative process and the use of the arts than any other source, because in it are found the great truths about man as well as God that are the wellsprings of art."[6]

2. Halley, *Halley's Bible Handbook*, 58.

3. Brueggemann, *Theology of the Old Testament*, 156.

4. Luther, "Open Letter."

5. Fee and Stuart, *How to Read the Bible*, 78.

6. Luther, "Open Letter."

The Bible reveals God in the form of story, poetry, dreams and images, all of which open new understanding and meaning. It is littered with metaphor, symbolism, narrative and parable. There is an abundance of metaphors used to describe God: light, water, rock, fire, wind. Terence Fretheim writes that these terms evoke wonder and awe in human beings. The use of natural metaphors for God opens up the entire created order as a resource for depth and variety in God-language.[7]

McKnight quotes Anthony Thistleton: "If metaphor presents possibility rather than actuality it is arguable that metaphoric discourse can open up new understanding more readily than purely descriptive or scientific statement."[8] Using metaphor opens the imagination, creating pictures that enable connection with the Creator. Stanley Hauerwas suggests that art, like metaphor, is first and foremost a way of talking, a way of thinking, a way of using language to make sense of God, the world and ourselves.[9] Once a person finds their place in that story they are able to connect others to the greater story of redemption. If a Christ-follower can invite an unchurched person to share their story, it opens up an opportunity to bring a missional connection. This is a nonthreatening, natural way to create an opportunity to bring Jesus into conversation.

Jesus connected with the culture of his day in a way they understood. He condensed the Decalogue into two easy-to-understand commands. He had a way of speaking to the heart of humanity, from all walks of life. He simplified the complex and spoke not only a language that the people understood, but moved them to change, or at the very least see the state they were in. He captured the imagination of his listeners through narratives, parables and metaphors that painted a spiritual reality.

Scot McKnight states that the church does not find God in speculative thinking but rather in the life and work of a person.[10]

7. Fretheim, *God and World*, 257.

8. McKnight, *Community Called Atonement*, 37.

9. Hauerwas, *Performing the Faith*, 83.

10. McKnight et al., *Church in the Present Tense*, 33.

Jesus' teachings are full of examples where he painted pictures with his descriptions of the fox, the sparrow, the dove, the lily, the vines, vineyards, trees and seeds. Jesus was a master storyteller. He related stories of rich men and poor people, of struggling widows and wealthy people of power and position. He made use of his own cultural setting to impart his message. Many of the parables were fictional, but were used to teach spiritual truths via the imagination.

According to Colin Harbinson, the church today must celebrate its own story and creatively show it to a word-weary and biblically illiterate world.[11] In postmodern Australia, the Bible is not the common book that people reach for to make sense of their life or answer their questions. Google is the preferred option. Art can be used to reach a person, to respond to questions or to begin to ask questions. People can be encouraged to tell their stories on canvas. Stories can be drawn out, questions discovered. This is an opportunity for connection with God to occur.

Imagination, sometimes referred to as the faculty of imagining, is a part of God's design. It plays a key role in learning.[12] Image-making serves as a powerful vehicle for expressing truth. The Bible repeatedly appeals to the intelligence through imagination. This finds its practice in the production or creation of artwork.

Art often speaks subliminally, or subconsciously, beyond awareness. This kind of information supersedes cognitive reasoning. In that regard, art—poetry, music, painting, dance—assists the onlooker to gain insight, to see beyond what can be seen with the eye; it has the ability to open up a curiosity within. Even those who have not connected with their creativity can have an appreciation of what is made or created. Sayers wrote, "The words of creeds come before our eyes and ears as pictures."[13] The mind takes the words and an image forms. God consistently uses stories to create images by which people learn; there is no need to explain

11. Harbinson, "Restoring the Arts to the Church."

12. Egan, *Imagination in Teaching and Learning*, 50.

13. Sayers, "Mind of the Maker," 20.

imagery. The learning happens unconsciously and often a spiritual connection is made.

Creativity is wrapped up in identity. John Holden writes, "In the post-modern world people define themselves not so much by their jobs, because they come and go, not so much by geography, because people commute and move around. It is more by cultural consumption and production. I am who I am, and you are who you are, because of what we watch, read, listen to, write and play."[14] In light of this, culture influences lives as much as location, vocation or any other activity.

Friedhelm Mennekes asserts, "The artist's role is to disturb the way to understand a sacred space. They disturb everything by questioning and this is so important. Being into art, opening your mind to art, is questioning, questioning as existentialism."[15] Art in itself is a practical form of questioning. The artist really has to ask practical questions in order to create. So in this way its form is spiritual openness.

There are intrinsic qualities and skills associated with painting that are fundamentally valuable to social dialogue. Artist Eve Stafford believes that art is the most powerful weapon available to change perceptions, because it uses symbolism and metaphor. The strength of art-making is its capacity to communicate in multisensory or emotional domains.[16] Not only does it communicate, but it touches something deep within the person creating it and can reach beyond to those who look upon it.

Stafford adds, "A voice, or expression is a big part of being heard. The art is about remaking and recreating ourselves. We start from where we are and with what we've got. The biggest resource is personal experiences, our stories, our life-skills, and our creativity."[17] If we as Christ-followers and artists can connect a person with their creative side and then connect that with their story and in turn connect their story with the spiritual questions, then

14. Holden, "How We Value Arts," 447.
15. Mennekes, "Art of Spirituality."
16. See Stafford, "CCD."
17. Stafford, "CCD," 16–20.

God can be revealed. Ian Maxwell and Fiona Winning state that "ultimately art is 'experienced' by the maker/s, but also by spectators and appreciators. So as a story is told and uncovered on canvas it connects also with those looking on."[18]

Art is such a powerful medium. Mack Hicks, in *Psychology Today*, writes that the left brain's focus is on detail and control. The right brain is open to new experiences and brings us the richness of imagination and creativity. Both sides of our brain are involved in our thoughts and behaviors, but some of us rely on characteristics of one side of the brain more than the other. This difference gives us a wholly distinct take on the world.[19] If we can encourage a person to extend time in right-brain pursuits, this can be of great benefit to an individual. I believe that right-brain activities can greatly assist us to process life and even begin to question different ways of thinking. This can in turn open up opportunities for individuals to consider things of a more spiritual nature.

Mihaly Csikszentmihalyi, in his book *Flow*, writes about the phenomenology of enjoyment. He refers to a state of *flow*. He writes that one dimension of the flow experience is that, while it lasts, one is able to forget all the unpleasant aspects of life. The enjoyable activity requires a complete focusing of attention on the task at hand—thus leaving no room in the mind for irrelevant information.[20] This is what I have witnessed when people are involved in painting. Csikszentmihalyi continues that in normal everyday existence, we are the prey of thoughts and worries that intrude into our consciousness.[21] With depression and anxiety, often these thoughts consume much of a person's time. If we can encourage a person to experience *flow* this takes the pressure off, even if only for a short time.

Csikszentmihalyi further describes the state of flow as, "The state in which people are so involved in an activity that nothing

18. Maxwell and Winning, "Towards a Critical Practice," 8–20.
19. Hicks, "Who Stole the Right Side of Your Brain?"
20. Csikszentmihalyi, *Flow*, 58.
21. Ibid.

else seems to matter."[22] Further to this he states, "The safest generalization to make about this phenomenon is to say that during the flow experience the sense of time bears little relation to the passage of time as measured by the absolute convention of the clock."[23] Again, this is a constant response from those engaging in the painting section of Art and Soul, the common theme that the participants report is that they "lose themselves in the painting experience" or that they lose all concept of time. Many report that they feel they have only been painting for a short time and yet the period of time is much greater.[24]

Neuroscientist David Creswell goes a step further. He says that in order to gain an insight, it is helpful for an individual to completely change the thought process. He explains that the brain regions that were active when the initial information was given about the problem continue to be active when the brain is distracted with another task—he refers to this as unconscious neural reactivation.[25]

Art and Soul delivers the information, the person then engages in the painting, which totally distracts them from the issue that they have been informed about, but their brain is still processing the information. The small group then allows the processing after the distraction, which seems to make it a lot more effortless and the benefits apparent.

Crewell's thesis is that when trying to solve a complex task, people who were distracted after first tackling the problem did better than people who put in conscious effort. He says that letting go of the need for your own conscious mind to do all the problem solving might be the key. He encourages the individual to let the unconscious do more work, whether through napping or distractions; this could include painting. He states that it may cause an individual to become more effective in problem solving.[26]

22. Ibid., 4.
23. Ibid., 66.
24. Ware, qualitative research evaluation.
25. Cited in Rock, "Stop Trying to Solve Problems."
26. Ibid.

Finally, Csikszentmihalyi speaks about the concept of flow having eight major components. When people reflect on how it feels, they mention at least one, and often all, of the following:

1. We confront tasks we have a chance of completing;
2. We must be able to concentrate on what we are doing;
3. The task has clear goals;
4. The task provides immediate feedback;
5. One acts with deep, but effortless involvement, that removes from awareness the worries and frustrations of everyday life;
6. One exercises a sense of control over their actions;
7. Concern for the self disappears, yet, paradoxically the sense of self emerges stronger after the flow experience is over; and
8. The sense of duration of time is altered.

He states that the combination of all these elements causes a sense of deep enjoyment that is so rewarding people feel that expending a great deal of energy is worthwhile simply to be able to feel it.[27] Most, if not all, of these are present in the Art and Soul experience.

27. Csikszentmihalyi, *Flow*, 58.

5

Kaleidoscope: A Faith Community

I HAD ALWAYS THOUGHT that I was focused outside of the church. I ran many (attractional) outreach events. They were great, but in reality they were only touching a very small part of the population. I remember driving to work in 2009; I had been on staff at the church for over ten years at this stage. The church consisted of about 150 people when I arrived and had grown to about twelve hundred in those years. In Australia, this is a large church.

This was a difficult time for me. Each morning as I drove to work, I would cry. The question that kept forming on my lips was: What are we doing? What are we doing? On different days there was an emphasis on a different word, but the question remained the same. Nothing was wrong, but I was stirred to do something different.

In 2010 we planted Kaleidoscope. I need to say Kaleidoscope is not *the* answer. It is a response. There are many, many things that are not working well. I am constantly reevaluating and trying to work things out. It really is an exploration. And it has been a really difficult journey. But it has been fun. I have found the fun in ministry again.

Kaleidoscope sits within a unique culture and demographic. Kaleidoscope is a Greek word: *kalos* means "beautiful," *eidos* means "form," and *scope* means "to look at."[1] This is what the church should be, a beautiful form, which, when the light, Jesus, shines through it, creates a different picture wherever it is seen. This image of church may look different to other depictions of church, but it should be beautiful in form. Each Sunday afternoon the Kaleidoscope community gathers together to create a church for the unchurched. These gatherings are intended to not only build community, but create a place for people to explore spirituality. Everything in these meetings is geared around creating missional conversations and exploring spirituality with one another in the community but also a strong focus on the unchurched.

Church culture is deeply ingrained in so many areas, language, behavior, and thought processes. After being in the church culture for a period of time it is difficult to see it for what it is. There are often various cultural practices that insiders call doctrine that are possibly more practice and methodology than tenets of the faith. One area that occurs but is often unseen is the use of religious jargon; it is often quite different from what is used in everyday life. When we started Kaleidoscope we realized how much jargon we used. We had to relearn to speak in nonreligious language. We introduced a "swear jar" to address this; but instead of fines for swearing, the fines were imposed for using religious jargon. I got the first two fines in the community.

In many cases we needed to deconstruct to be able to reconstruct worship in a new form. Kaleidoscope began to explore different forms of worship, including painting, creative writing, contemplation, conversation and service. I think in many instances we have reduced the power of the church to a very structured and sometimes sedate form that hates interruption.

Over the last eight or nine months there has been a man attending Kaleidoscope whose life has been really tough. Max looks a little rough around the edges. He plays a little with art and may even call himself an artist. He has had a stroke and walks with a

1. Dictionary.reference.com, s.v. "kaleidoscope."

stick and arrives in a fairly unkempt condition. He has been so rude to me over the months. He comes and eats the meal and drinks the wine and has consistently refused to sit through the "God part," telling us that he is a confirmed atheist; he used to attend atheist meetings in the city every Sunday.

A few weeks ago he arrived an hour late. He did not realize that it was daylight savings. He came in, walked up to me, and said, "Well, where's the food?" I asked him to sit down and told him I would get him some. He replied, "I'm not sitting here listening to the God stuff, I'll go up to the dining part." I told him that he couldn't go up there, as a group of people were cleaning up, and the children's program was being run up there, as well. I told him that he needed to sit down, that John would get him some wine, and I would get him a meal. He sat down and for the first time sat through a whole meeting.

Two weeks later it was a long weekend and about half of the community had gone away camping, and so it was a very small gathering with only approximately thirty adults, a few kids and teenagers, so on this night we were all eating pizza in the meeting area rather than in the dining section. Again he was forced to sit in with us. Levi was speaking and I was scheduled on painting. At the end of the message, I got up to share my painting. Max walked up to me as I begin to talk, pointed to the microphone in my hand, and said, "Put that thing down. Put that down for a minute." I obeyed. He said, "This is the first time I've put my two bob's worth in"—an Australian colloquialism for contributing to the conversation. I was quite surprised by this. He must have seen the surprise on my face. I told him that was a really positive thing. He then said, "Do you know why I put my two bob's worth in?" As I shook my head, he said, "It's because I feel accepted." I asked him if I could share that with the rest of the community. He agreed, and as I told them, he walked out of the door with a wave. Each week now, Max sits with us and contributes his "two bob's worth." What occurred to me was that if Max did that in many other structured church forums, walked up to the pastor and told them to put the microphone down, he would be ushered out by the deacons, because the form has become so important. I am not saying that this is how we should run the church services. I think this sort of disruption on a regular basis would need to be addressed. But sometimes we can miss what is occurring in an individual's life because the focus is on the church service being the most important thing.

McNeal notes that the church in the New Testament is disruptive, organic, personal, prophetic, kingdom-focused, with empowering leadership.[2] The church, *ecclesia*—those called out—was always used to speak of people. It was not referring to a building. It also identifies their gathering to worship and serve the Lord. Missional ministry is focused on taking the church to the people rather than bringing people to the church.

In the Australian context, even more so than many other countries, the less structured and more relaxed style of gatherings are more in keeping with the culture. With a new church plant, the vision and possibility of what might be, rather than what is, drives the methodology. Structure is not as necessary. Risk is prized, creativity embraced, and people are encouraged to be involved. Fluidity is so much simpler as change is not too deeply imbedded. Evaluating what works and what does not is more important than deep-seated, structured practice. Acts 20—the story of Eutychus falling asleep and falling out of the third story window and being raised from death to life—gives a picture of an unstructured meeting where the Spirit of God was evident.

One of the core values of the community: Kaleidoscope is a community of ordinary people who seek to value tradition, while embracing innovation, risk, and the possibility of failure for the sake of one another and for those not yet a part of the community. I believe that we need to be willing to risk for the sake of those who are not yet a part of our community; if we do not these people may never realize that they have that opportunity to be included in community. The journey is not one of seeking comfort. A catch-cry of the early Kaleidoscope community became, "Comfort Diminishes

2. These ideas are a summation of statements made by McNeal in *Present Future*.

Passion." This is so true; if I am seeking my comfort, those things that I am passionate about will become just a dull ache.

The focus of Kaleidoscope is on attempting to move people out into community rather than trying to get unchurched people into meetings. Once this occurs the idea is to create a place that is easy to approach with few boundaries preventing people from entering. These gatherings are an easy entrance point in the form of a Sunday meeting for the unchurched to attend, with people then moving from Sunday to Tuesday evening meetings, where there are more familiar components of church services, including communion, worship in the form of singing and deeper teaching. The mission of the church is not to get people into the sacred place. Sacred dwells within the believer and is carried out to the community. Believers embody the message; in a sense Christians are the message.

Hirsch writes, "If discipleship making lies at the heart of our commission then we must organize it around mission, because mission is the catalyzing principle of discipleship. In Jesus they are inexorably linked."[3] This needs to be how that is lived out, not just something tacked onto the end. Hirsch adds, "If we wish to develop and engender a genuinely missional leadership, then we have to first plant the seed of obligation to the mission of God in the world in the earlier and more elementary phases of discipleship."[4] This flows from the heart of the community. It cannot be taught; it must be practiced.

Over the years, the emphasis in many churches has shifted from conversion to a salvation moment. many come and put their hands up to receive Jesus but are just as quickly exiting the building. Creating community and discipleship needs to be intentional.

Webber contrasts the conversion of Constantine and Justin Martyr. He states that Constantine's conversion appeared to be rote and mechanical, following the rules but missing the Spirit. Martyr's was more connected to an experience.[5] The gospel message is

3. Hirsch, *Forgotten Ways*, 189.
4. Hirsch, *Forgotten Ways*, 119.
5. Webber, *Ancient-Future Evangelism*, 25.

more than the transfer of information. It needs the empowerment of the Holy Spirit, but it is questionable whether the emotion-charged altar lines are the best alternative.

In many cases salvation has become a moment in time, whereas conversion is a process in which, in many instances, discipleship has been omitted. The Sunday meeting is central but relational aspects are often missing. It in some cases has become a very compartmentalized approach to Christianity. This carries over into other areas—often if people are involved in worship, they cannot be involved in mission. They often find their area of ministry and leave mission to the evangelists. The focus must be on every person connecting with the people in their world.

Webber writes that conversion is not merely embracing an intellectual idea; it is taking one's place within the body of people who confess Christ and seek to live out the kingdom of Jesus.[6] What has been affective in the past may not be the best way forward. The church has an unchanging message in a changed world. It needs to be communicated in a new cultural context. Christian formation takes place in community. The final part of this is for people to discover their gifts and serve. The process of evangelism is slow and less segmented or compartmentalized than has been done in the past. It is a process that requires community. This involves engaging with people and generating missional conversations.

Carson states that a missional engagement requires immersion in culture, to listen and ask questions. A missionary then proposes responses from the gospel, rather than attempting to impose a message.[7] The place to begin is to inquire as to what strategies will better reflect our postmodern situation; to look for connection points. It is important to recognize what questions are being asked and what conversations are being spoken. Often the church tries and responds to questions that are not being asked, giving the rolled-out, pat answer that Christians have been famous for.

Recently three young men arrived at Kaleidoscope. They asked who we were and what we were doing. After telling them

6. Ibid, 39.

7. Carson, *Becoming Conversant*, 62.

that we were a church, their response was that we did not look like a church, we could not be a proper, full-blown church. They revealed that they were practicing pagans. I asked them where they met; they answered, around a bonfire. They wanted to know what a church meeting at Kaleidoscope looked like. After explaining how the evening meeting would run, they asked if they could stay and hear about the Bible. At the end of the night they stated that they thought that we had a lot of similar beliefs. We looked at points of similarity of belief and then began to speak about points of difference. Their view of what church is and their understanding of it were so totally foreign to what we adhere to. These three young men have attended sporadically ever since and have even visited our Tuesday night church meetings. These men's opinion of church prevented them from entertaining even a thought to visit a church. It was by accident that they came, but they are beginning to discover a community where they can explore the gospel and find answers to their questions. Recently one of them converted to Christianity.

In many ways we need to relearn to connect and communicate to the culture, to make an effort to form relationships outside the church that were once effortless. In the New Testament church there was a strong focus on community, caring and loving and contributing all together (Acts 2:32), as well as a call to social justice and compassion for the suffering and destitute.[8] The disciples heard Jesus talk about the kingdom and were willing to engage the world.

Art holds a prominent place in the Kaleidoscope community. Art can be a very individual pursuit. Kaleidoscope desires to create a place for artists to form community. We are looking to create a place for the expression of painting and other art mediums. To encourage people to create, relate and release the creative within them, as well as to provide places where art can be displayed and shared. Not all are artists, but everyone can appreciate the story or expression of art. The sermon is spoken and also painted. An aspect of the message is revealed through artwork. It shows a

8. Horton, *Systematic Theology*, 543.

different form and often a different view of the message being preached. It often awakens something in those looking on. Steve Turner, in his book *Imagine*, writes, "A sermon requires authority, clarity and a personal challenge. Art on the other hand, often deals in doubt, ambiguity and self-criticism."[9]

Often there is a prophetic element in the paintings, which is able to minister quite deeply to the participants or those looking on. As the Sunday meetings are designed around the unchurched community and creating a place for them to explore spirituality, art is a good medium for this to occur. Several unchurched people have attended Kaleidoscope and found painting a nonthreatening entrance to the church meeting. There are tables set for others to paint or involve themselves in other forms of art. A contemplative table is also available where people can sit and look through photography books or write in journals.

There are many unchurched artists who have been a part of this journey whose lives have been impacted and connected with Jesus. One artist who has been involved in painting in the community has stepped up into an art-teaching role in Patmos, and has attended Kaleidoscope to paint. She heard the message of the Beatitudes and painted a picture of the mountain with darkness around the edges, she glued words such as darkness, war, blame and discord along the edges. She was invited to share the story of her painting at Kaleidoscope, to which she responded, "Jesus spoke a message from the mountain that was bringing hope and light into a hurt and pained world." Here we had an unchurched person sharing the message of Jesus to the church. She is continuing to impact and be impacted through this story.

Craig Detweiler, in his book *Unchristian*, writes, "We have become famous for what we oppose rather than whom we are for."[10] The church should be known for what it does, reaching out to the poor, helping the needy and alleviating suffering. Art and social justice often have a base connection. Turner notes, "Art is created from passion and when artists are passionate about injustice or

9. Turner, *Imagine*, 55.

10. Detweiler, *Unchristian*, 17.

persecution it is almost inevitable that it will affect their work."[11] Because of this, many with an artistic bent have a desire to assist the poor and needy. This spills over into the Art for Justice initiative. McNeal writes that "the church is a club for religious people where club members can celebrate their traditions and hang out with others who share common thinking and lifestyles. They do not automatically think of the church as championing the cause of poor people or healing the sick or serving people."[12] Sadly they do not realize the church desires to respond to these issues. There are many in the outside community who are drawn to a cause and want to contribute to make the world a better place to live or give a voice to those who are voiceless. There are many people interested in being involved in advocacy and the raising of awareness and funds for a worthwhile cause. Thus Kaleidoscope is seeking to provide opportunities for these people to join us.

Brian McLaren, in *Everything Must Change*, writes, "The church has specialized in people's destination in the afterlife but has failed to address significant social injustices in this life. It has focused on 'me' and 'my soul' and 'my spiritual life' and 'my eternal destiny,' but it has failed to address the dominant societal and global realities of their lifetime: systemic injustice, systemic poverty, systemic ecological crisis."[13] There seems to be an awakening to this within the church in recent times, at least acknowledging the issues in many cases. Kaleidoscope desires to focus on some of these social issues. While recognizing that the afterlife is important, the world can be affected here and now, suffering can be alleviated, lives can be impacted during this lifetime.

The larger focus of Kaleidoscope is to create and develop intersecting points with the community. the majority of people in the community will never step inside a church.

11. Turner, *Imagine*, 52.

12. McNeal, *Present Future*, 11.

13. McLaren, *Everything Must Change*, 19.

6

Art for Justice: Going into the Marketplace

JULIE IS A SCHOOL teacher. She wandered up to the Art for Justice stall at the market and watched us paint. As we talked she began to ask about Art and Soul. Julie was fascinated with the Art and Soul program. I explained to her what it was and how it ran. Julie invited us into her class to run some sessions with her classes. We conducted an Art and Soul session on identity, with 180 children over four days. It was wonderful. From this Julie decided to participate in the Art and Soul class herself. She is now attending our monthly painting nights. We have had the most wonderful conversations with her about Jesus. She realizes that God is at work in her life. She is open to coming to Kaleidoscope.

In the following pages I will begin to introduce a few strategies of using art to generate missional conversations in the community. The chapter will detail Art for Justice; taking art and music into the literal market place; raising money and awareness of a social justice needs while creating opportunities for missional conversations and relationships.

There is an interest in many pockets of Australia for people to be involved in a cause. Many unchurched people want to have an impact in their world, but are unsure how to go about it. Many people volunteer time and money to a cause that is beyond them.[1] Several people have connected to the Kaleidoscope community through different social justice activities and events.

Art for Justice is a deliberate attempt to move into the literal market place. It creates a reason to go into the local market and generate conversations with people who are not in church. Art for Justice also creates a place for people with a love of art or music to gather together in a community atmosphere. Many are drawn to the cause, and that creates conversations with people that would not otherwise be possible. There are others who are not so interested in the cause but love the music or the art.

There are several unchurched groups within the Art for Justice Days that are a part of the target audience. The first group is those that come and are a part of the Art for Justice team. The second group is the visitors at the market. Both of these groups are where Kaleidoscope looks to generate missional conversations. This is a slow, deliberate journey and it is emphasized that the conversations and sharing of the gospel not be rushed.

The strategy is to invite spectators or those working with us on team to come on a journey. The team consists of artists who paint, musicians who play music, or those who work the fair-trade stall, as well as random people who decide to turn up on the day; we have had face-painters, masseurs and jugglers as just a few examples of extras that turn up to be involved with us. Often these people are not followers of Christ; but this gives more opportunities and options to engage in ongoing conversation. It normalizes relationships and many are open to attending Kaleidoscope after coming to an Art for Justice event. The end result is that people have the opportunity to commence or move further along the journey. Several have involved themselves further in the Kaleidoscope community from conversations that were held at the market.

Hundreds of people attend Arkoonah Market in Berwick, in Melbourne's southeastern suburbs. Sunday morning finds people wandering slowly around the market and many are open

1. Fundraising Institute Australia, "2012 Giving Trends Report."

to engaging in conversations. People are drawn by the music and interested in watching paintings emerge on canvas. It is easy to draw an audience and commence dialogue. People are generally open to contribute finance, whether it is a donation for the art and music in the form of busking or at times donations toward the social justice cause. Money is raised and the social justice cause itself draws conversations.

Connection with people is as diverse as the individuals involved. We look to connect with anyone visiting the market. Many of the people who stop and engage in conversation are interested in looking at the artwork being produced. Frequently people who paint are drawn to a community of artists and want to find out more about what is going on and how they can be involved.

Art can be quite an individual pursuit. It is often seen as a rather self-indulgent pastime. Creating opportunity for artists to contribute to a cause beyond themselves and engage in community activities, particularly one related to a social justice cause, is often attractive to an artist.

Artists involved in Art for Justice do not need to have well-developed skills or hold a qualification. All they need is to be prepared to paint with people looking on. The aim is more to create a sense of community and interest in what is occurring rather than painting a masterpiece. Many of the participants of the Art and Soul course are happy to attend the Art for Justice days. This gives another entrance point on the journey for Kaleidoscope to engage in missional conversations with them.

Art for Justice also provides musicians with a place to play with other musicians they would normally not interact with. Musicians who have no public place to play are drawn to this event. There is usually a spare guitar or some bongos for any spontaneous visitor to join in. Musicians need to be raw and organic and it helps to understand the cause. They need to be able to connect quickly with others and feel comfortable with impromptu performance. The art and music sets an atmosphere and causes a synergy to occur within the group. The sense of camaraderie is quite profound. Frequently, artists and musicians ask if they can be involved in this event and in some instances are interested in being involved in other areas of music and art at Kaleidoscope and other projects.

The next group of people are those who love a cause. The people on our team assist with the fair-trade stall. The stall sells jewelry and other items made in the slums of Bangkok. On some occasions we have sold fair-trade coffee beans at the stall. There are quite a few people interested in fair-trade issues, others have no idea what fair trade is but are interested to find out more. This creates an easy talking point for many of the market-goers. However, it is often the specific social justice project that causes the most conversations. Often there are just people who are curious as to what is going on. The whole point is not a hard sell or an open intent to witness to people but often to invite them to another point on the journey.

We have three main organizations that we support. The first is GraceWorks.[2] Anthony and Vicki Ware are members at Kaleidoscope and partners in running this organization in Myanmar. They are seeing amazing things occur in this country, improving opportunities and quality of life for people in Myanmar. The second organization is Abolishion, headed up by Leanne Rhodes.[3] I am a board member of Abolishion and believe strongly in what we are doing. It is an anti-human trafficking organization that operates in Romania and Moldova, particularly involved in breaking the systems that keep people in sexual slavery. The third organization is Operation Hope, directed by Chris and Fiona Grech, who are also members of the Kaleidoscope community. They operate mainly in Swaziland, empowering the people to improve their lifestyle in an impoverished community. Chris and Fiona spend their time between there and Australia.

One of the main social justice projects that we sponsor through Art for Justice is the Sister Act Project, run by Operation Hope.[4] In developing countries, millions of girls are unable to afford sanitary pads. This forces them to miss three to five

2. graceworksmyanmar.org.au.
3. abolishion.org.
4. operationhopeinc.org.au/sisteract.

days of school during their monthly periods, and many eventually drop out, which compromises their education and ultimately their future. Girls often resort to using old cloth, pieces of mattress, and other materials that promote infection and leak, causing embarrassment. Lack of education almost always leads to a lifetime of social and economic vulnerability, and many uneducated girls turn to prostitution or early marriage, putting them at greater risk of contracting HIV/AIDS and other diseases, particularly in a polygamist society like Swaziland, which has the highest prevalence of HIV in the world.

Operation Hope has created a way to help girls in developing countries stay in school—helping them manage menstruation. Extensive research is showing that if girls continue in school, they will marry later, have fewer children, but most importantly, invest 90 percent of their income back into their families, compared to only 30–40 percent for men, thereby not just transforming their home but also their community. If these girls stay in school they are three times less likely to become HIV positive.[5]

Interventions like Operation Sister Act are a cost-effective way of keeping girls in school. This project seeks to encourage women in developed countries like Australia to empower young girls living in poverty to become the women they were called to be. Operation Hope has sourced kits, which are now being produced in Swaziland, for the Swazi girls. Each kit, costing $20AUD, is packed with reusable sanitary napkins (that last up to eighteen months) and other essential sanitation products, including soap, underwear and life-saving information on HIV/AIDS prevention.

We take one of these kits and set this up on the fair-trade stall. It creates many conversations with people interested in contributing and a desire to know more about the cause. Over the years many kits have been purchased and much money given toward this cause. The production and distribution of the packs make a difference in individual lives and in turn their communities. It

5. See ibid.

also makes a difference to those that run the small business that produces the packs. People in Australia are willing to support the cause by donating money, and it is quite easy to engage in conversation with the market-goers on these issues, which often leads to further conversations on where and how can they be involved.

At the market we have made many interesting connections. At one of the Art for Justice events we met seven people, at different stages throughout the day, who all stated that either they used to paint or would love to paint but just didn't find time. We invited these people to a casual, painting night. This is held in a garage with a loose theme chosen to converse around and paint. This worked really well and so we have continued to run them on a monthly basis.

On this first painting night we served mulled wine, and I spoke briefly about transitions and changes in our lives and we painted on the theme of change. One of the men that attended related that his wife had passed away twelve months previously and he was struggling to come to terms with her death and his loss. He attended several painting nights. Although he did not attend church or become a Christ follower, a relationship began and a conversation was started.

These painting nights now run on a monthly basis. This is just a very lightly structured painting get-together. There is no deliberate instruction although the participants assist one another with thoughts and ideas. The evening is conducted with a very relaxed atmosphere and conversation. The feedback is that these conversations usually connect with a need in at least some of the participant's lives.

Tricky Paul was another one of the seven that we met that morning at Art for Justice. He attended several painting nights. He is a fascinating character. He kept walking around painting on other people's paintings as well as his own. That's why I gave him the name Tricky Paul. It took a while to work him out. He is raising his grandchild, as his daughter is heavily involved in drugs. Tricky Paul works as a social worker for an organization dealing with people who suffer depression. He has sent many caseworkers to Art and Soul over the time that we have known him.

These are two meaningful relationships that began from a simple conversation in the market place. So people move from Art for Justice to the random painting nights to Art and Soul, or from Art and Soul to the painting nights and Art for Justice; they all somehow link together to form relationships with people who would not go to a church.

7

Art and Soul: Teaching People Who Suffer from Depression and Anxiety to Paint

LEANNE ATTENDED THE VERY first Art and Soul course.[1] My journey with her has been quite deep and significant. She had lost her grandmother about three months before commencing the course. When I met her she related the story about how her partner's car ran out of fuel. As he was pushing the car to the service station, he had a heart attack, collapsed and died. Leanne was struggling dealing with the loss of two very significant people in her life within a short space of time.

On week eight of the course, the faith and spirituality night, there is a section where I ask the participants to close their eyes and allow the music being played to impact them. When Leanne closed her eyes and listened to the music, she saw herself walking down a road; as she walked she came to a fork in the road. She related that as she arrived at that point, God reached out to take her hand and lead her forward. She was quite emotional. In the following moments, I asked my small group to take their visual diaries

1. artandsoul.org.au.

and write at the top of the page the word "Dear," followed by their name. Then I told them that God wanted to speak to them and asked them to begin to write. They all exchanged looks as though I was asking them to do something very foreign, but one by one they began to write a letter to themselves from God.

When Leanne began to write her letter she recounted that God began to tell her how much he loved her and how beautiful she was to him. He then told her that it was time to leave the things of the past behind; he had a new road for her to take. This was a deep emotional moment for her. From here Leanne began to visit Kaleidoscope and earlier this year I officiated the wedding of her and her new partner. She is still on a journey of discovery, but this particular session opened up the opportunity for that journey to commence.

In the following pages I will continue to build on strategies of using art to connect with the community. The chapter will introduce Art and Soul, a course that I developed as a part of my doctorate at Fuller. Art and Soul is a ten-week course that combines art with teaching, and group discussions can be used to explore thinking and emotions that lead to depression and anxiety. Within the course there is a faith and spirituality lesson that builds onto the discussions from the previous weeks to a point where we create a space and conversation for Jesus to reveal himself.

People do not naturally assume that a church is where they want to find spiritual fulfillment. Often a person considers that the church is a place where they will be judged for poor choices or lifestyle options. Art does not judge. It does not condemn. It reveals what is, whether seen or unseen. It does not work through a cognitive process but displays what is under the surface. Art can move a person to tears or even laughter. It is not seen as a religious or evangelistic enterprise, so people are open to explore and converse.

Art creates a place for stories to be told. It is usually a non-threatening form of questioning and story telling. In turn this can lead to conversations about life, significance, purpose and pain. In time this may lead to the bigger question of faith and God. Art and Soul gives an opening for people to connect with God.

Those who have participated in Art and Soul have been many and varied. There has been no trouble attracting people to the Art and Soul course. The initial group of twenty-one participants came through a newspaper article. The following courses recruited people mainly though word of mouth.

Depression and anxiety are large issues in the local community.[2] Most people who have attended Art and Soul are not those who have had a deep-seated mental illness. More often it is people who have suffered tragedies and are trying to work their way forward. The people who have participated in Art and Soul have stated that there are not a lot of places for people to process their issues of life, and sadly, church is not always a safe place that they readily turn to.[3]

In the local demographic, the southeastern suburbs of Melbourne, Australia, where we commenced Art and Soul, there is a large and growing rate of depression and anxiety. After four years of running Art and Soul with well over two hundred participants, several people that have attended classes have suffered the loss of a loved one, or have suffered trauma or tragedy of some sort. Many of these people find that the Art and Soul group provides that place for them to process their circumstances.

Several of the participants that suffer from anxiety or depression desperately want to move forward but are unsure how to begin. Many of them have been in a situation for quite some time and feel that they are stuck or caged. Often they do not need much encouragement to help them move. Most of them had a desire to learn to paint. There have also been many who are not particularly interested in art but want to understand themselves more.

Because of the high incidence of depression and anxiety within the community, there is an openness to engage in courses and even conversations that may bring some relief. A ten-week course gives time for people to learn some basic art and painting

2. Kitchener and Jorm, *Youth Mental Health*, 11.

3. Ware, qualitative research evaluation.

skills and to be able to produce enough artwork for an exhibition. The ten-week timeframe also gives opportunity for people to develop a love for painting.

More than this, it allows the opportunity for participants to connect with others and begin to look at life issues, engage in conversation and develop relationships. Many conversations regarding God and spirituality have commenced and many are ongoing. It creates the possibility for those involved to continue painting. We recently filmed the classes so that other groups could begin to implement the program.

The nine themes that make up Art and Soul—Identity, Core Beliefs, Power and Shame, Holistic Health, Loss and Grief, Emotions, Connections, Faith and Spirituality, and Celebration—cover major areas of life. People who suffer depression and anxiety can relate to these topics so it was important to create themes relevant to the audience. Each class begins with a twenty-minute teaching session, followed by a ninety-minute painting exercise. The participants complete an entire painting each week. The evening concludes with a half-hour small group discussion around the theme of the night. The small group discussions are an essential part of the course. Often the participants do not have a place to process the issues in their lives. Sometimes they have isolated themselves and other times they do not want to weigh down relationships with their problems. Sometimes relationships have worn thin from their constant conversations of depression and anxiety. The other participants in these groups are going through similar issues and it gives them a place to be honest about what is happening in their lives. It also normalizes some of their responses from which they may experience shame.

One lady whose mother and daughter had died within a three-week period was so ashamed as she shared about wanting to lash out at other happy families. Another member of the group whose son had died spoke of experiencing the same emotions. The woman who had shared about this had never verbalized it before and had lived with terrible guilt over these feelings. This small group discussion greatly assisted her to be able to speak those feelings out and realize that others had experienced the same emotions. She was not an evil person, she was just experiencing grief. The small group is where the most profound missional conversations occur. The week eight topic, faith and spirituality, is tailored to direct these conversations to commence.

The first session is on identity. The teaching session speaks to the fact that often an individual's identity may be built on false foundations. For example, "I might be warm and friendly, but if I am overweight I may believe that it cancels out the value of my friendliness;" "I might be kind and caring but if I am shy, I do not think that my compassion has much worth." We also look at different problems with the way we see ourselves.

The first art exercise is a tonal painting, the participants are taught how to paint light and shadow, dark and light. We photographed Willow Tree figurines and printed them out in black and white. The painter uses black and white mixed into five different shades. This can be tied in with their life experience, the light and dark of life. The first exercise is done over two weeks and so covers identity and core beliefs.

The questions in the small group relate to how we see ourselves. Many people ignore the positive parts of their personality and focus on the negative. We look at this as well as looking at personal strengths and weaknesses. On this night we also invite the participants to write in their visual diary what they would like to get out of the course.

The second session on core beliefs follows along a similar vein. The core beliefs that a person has direct how they behave. Because a person believes in gravity, they will not jump out of a high-rise window. If someone believes that coffee wakes them up, they will not feel fully engaged until they have their first coffee of the morning. If a person thinks they are not clever, they will not answer questions. The problem is that people often believe things about themselves that someone else has told them. These opinions, if taken on as truth, hold a lot of power over a person. In light of this we all need to decide who we want to have that level of power and control in our lives. Can others give a more balanced view? A person's core beliefs greatly affect how they live their lives. Most people in the class can identify at least one area of these teaching sessions that they relate to.

In the small group each participant fills out a questionnaire, which helps them to identify some of their core beliefs. The questionnaire includes the following statements: I'll be accepted if I achieve; I need to be approved of by others to feel good about myself; I cannot let others down, I need to keep everyone happy. The participants identify areas that they may have a core belief that does not have a solid basis. These are discussed in the group.

The third theme for the course is on power and shame. This session looks at the difference between guilt and shame; guilt concerns something I did, shame concerns who I am. This session looks at people's responses to shame. It is often expressed in two extremes: getting small, not having an opinion, apologizing a lot, feeling like a bother; or getting big, using anger to make the feelings go away, intimidating or manipulating people. The third response is to disappear—this is played out in leaving relationships, quitting when thing get too difficult. The ultimate disappearing act is suicide. This week often can be quite confronting and there are often emails going back and forth between facilitators and participants and coffee dates made.

The art exercise that goes with this session is on how to draw perspective, making things appear at the front of the painting and disappear into the background. The students draw a fence along the side of a road heading toward mountains in the background. This exercise fits well with the night on power and shame, as shame can make a person feel small and power and control can be manifest in making a person big, which is at times expressed in anger. Students can identify their painting with their lives and the topic.

In the small group a questionnaire is passed to the participants. The purpose is to help identify areas of shame in the person's life. Some statements included in this are: We expect our loved ones to know what we need/feel; Arguments are played out in our head; We triangulate relationships through fear of being honest and transparent. The students are given a chart with an anchor of shame. The base of the anchor has words such as envy, abuse, and lack of boundaries. The shaft of the anchor shows the overall responses to shame. They are asked to identify which response is normal for them.

I recently conducted this session as the second of a two-part workshop with a group of eight teenagers in a local high school. There has been a spate of teenage suicides in our region and these particular children were seen as high risk. Their ages ranged from thirteen to seventeen. What was interesting with this group was their response to shame. Normally there would be the majority of people in a group who would respond by getting small, with one or two getting big; there might be one out of a group who would identify disappearing as their common reaction. In this group every single teenager identified disappearing as their preferred option. I was really affected by this. I had encouraged the well-being officer at the school to participate with the teenagers; we talked at length about the responses of the kids.

Week four is spent looking at holistic health. This session addresses the physical side of depression and anxiety. This is a very practical teaching session, covering issues such as diet, sleep, exercise and journaling. This is the first night that color is introduced to the painters. The students choose colors and paint an initial layer on their canvas. They then use masking tape to cover parts of their painting and then paint lines and swirls over the top. This process is repeated several times creating an abstract painting.

In the small groups the participants are encouraged to rate themselves one to ten for each area: physical, mental, emotional, spiritual. One means that they are doing extremely badly, ten means that they are doing exceptionally well. For each area they record their score in their visual diary. Group discussions focus on these areas and they explain their rating and why they scored that way.

Each person then chooses one area to work on for the week, setting realistic, achievable goals. For example, if they chose physical they may set a goal of walking four times per week. Or they may want to journal twice per week. Some of the goals in spirituality may be to look for a church, begin to pray, or connect with others with a faith. This is often the first night that faith issues are discussed. On many occasions people have been shocked at how low they scored in the spiritual area. It seems to be a very normal way to bring up issues of spirituality.

Week five covers the subject of loss and grief. This session addresses many areas of loss. It may not only be the death of a person, but it may be the loss of a job, or a friendship, or a dream that won't be achieved. Different signs of grief are described. Participants become aware that some of the issues and feelings that they experience may have to do with loss and grief. Shaun Tan's book *The Red Tree* is read at the end of the teaching session. This beautiful book speaks of hope after depression. The painting exercise centers on painting pictures from Tan's book.

In the small group the questions focus on each person's personal experience with loss or grief. A graph with a list of emotional responses to grief is handed to each person. They look at common reactions/responses that they relate to. This evening's discussion is around how they express anger. This may be avoidance, explosion, attack or many other ways. They are encouraged to talk about it. Discussion is around how they manage their anger and this leads to encouraging them to look at what strategies they could put in place to help deal with their anger in a more healthy manner. Examples such as journaling, walking, gardening, and painting are discussed.

In one of these groups I asked the participants how they normally expressed anger. One girl told me that she would climb on top of the roof of her house. I asked her what she did when she climbed up there. She responded that she thought about jumping. I said to her, "Have you ever considered going for a walk instead?" The following week when I was asking how their week had been she said she had gone for a long walk. I said to her that that was a better response, and asked how far she had gone. She told me she had walked for twelve kilometers. This is a better way for her to deal with her anger.

The session covering the topic on connections is held on week six. This session speaks about how humanity is designed for relationship, and looks at healthy and unhealthy relationships. It speaks about the benefit of being in community. It also looks at safe and unsafe people. It also covers assertiveness. Many people feel that they do not have power to state what they need or want.

The week six art component has changed several times. It is, however, some form of portrait painting. Usually this is in abstract form, often using mixed mediums. So words or parts of a face may be cut from magazines and glued onto the canvas. There are often items such as string, glitter, jewels or ribbons that are used to build up the picture. The paintings are usually quite colorful and often represent characteristics of the individual's life.

The questions covered in the small group center on characteristics of a healthy relationship. A sheet is given out with a list of healthy and unhealthy characteristics. This encourages the participant to look at their life and assess where their boundaries and interactions cross over with others. They look at the difficulty that they may have stating clearly what they want, being able to say no, being too rigid, as well as many other issues. They identify aspects about their relational health that may need to change. They are also encouraged to identify connections in their life that they may want to work on or celebrate.

Week seven covers the topic of emotions. Participants are encouraged to look at their emotional responses and learn about their reactions. We talk about anger being the easiest emotion to access. There is also some teaching on assertiveness. It is important for people with depression to be able to state their needs. We look at how to be assertive without being aggressive.

The art exercise developed for the night on emotions is a different style of painting. Instead of using a flat canvas, facemasks are used as a canvas. They are instructed to paint the outside of the mask in colors and styles of how they think that people see them. Painting the inside of the masks to represent how they see themselves is the second part of the exercise. The inside of their masks are often quite dark, representing what life is like for them behind their mask. Painting the masks is quite confronting. Even though it is difficult initially, students soon participate and the masks enable quite deep and authentic conversations to occur within small groups.

On this night, the group conversation centers on how they recognize and process their emotions. They also look at their communication style. They spend time identifying their emotions and identifying situations that they are challenged in being assertive. This session is completed with identifying different tools, such as music, journaling, talking, and walking, among others, and then developing strategies to help work out what they are feeling and how to help process their emotions.

Faith and spirituality is strategically placed in week eight. This session follows seven weeks of quite deep and meaningful themes. The students have opened up, made friends and connected with the leaders. They feel comfortable in their surroundings. The previous weeks' topics have included physical, emotional and mental aspects of depression. Session eight introduces the spiritual aspect of our lives. This session is not so much heavy teaching; I relate my own personal story, one of discovery of God. The session speaks of the fact that all are created with a desire for significance and impact, and that God has purpose for each individual. Spiritual connection is an inherent part of humanity and if that connection is not made something is missing. This teaching session opens up the opportunity for a spiritual connection to be made in the small group session at the end of the night.

The use of symbols is fitting for the faith and spirituality night. We invite some Kaleidoscope musicians to play live music for the class. They are encouraged to close their eyes and listen to the music and are given an opportunity to think of or consider a symbol. Symbols are often an important part of painting and often reveal or represent a story. This also leads well into the later small group session with the musicians also playing a part in that.

Throughout the evening the participants have heard my personal testimony of how God impacted and changed my life. Earlier in the evening they listened to music and were directed

to close their eyes and picture symbols. They have painted something quite meaningful to them. All of this comes to a climax in the small group.

The participants normally move into their small group in different areas of the building, but for the spirituality night they remain in the same room. I direct them to close their eyes and allow the music to touch their heart and spirit. They sit, allowing the music to soothe them. From here I ask them to take their visual diary and at the top of the page and write, "Dear," followed by their name. They are told that God wants to speak to them and they are directed to begin to write what God is saying to them. This may begin a little awkwardly, but as they start to write many insightful moments occur. At the end of group time, most of the participants share this very intimate moment, which has been profound. Several people have commenced a walk with Jesus as a result of the exercise.

In the previous class that we ran, one lady told me that she could not stay for the small group session, as she needed to get home early. I was disappointed but understood. I asked her if she could just stay for the first introduction part and then leave, as I wanted her to experience this night. She agreed. As I led them through the process she began to write her letter from God. After some time she looked up and said, "I do not want to leave this place. The peace I feel is overwhelming." Another lady in the group wrote two full pages and then said that she was going home to keep writing. I find it extremely profound to see what God does in these small groups.

On occasion there has been an adverse reaction, but even these have opened up conversation. Barbara reacted really strongly when asked to write her letter from God. She grew quite irate during this session. She began swearing and stomped out of the room. This was quite confronting. Earlier in the evening I had put an invitation to a Kaleidoscope Christmas party on her table. At this point I went to her table and removed the invitation.

At the end of the night, she came and apologized for her outburst and related the fact that she had been brought up in a fundamentalist Christian home and had vowed that she would never step foot inside a church again. She admitted that this God seemed very different from the God presented to her in her childhood. She told me that she had seen the invitation on the table and asked if she could have it. She consequently visited Kaleidoscope and invited several other participants of the Art and Soul course to attend as well. This conversation would not have occurred waiting for her to visit a church, as her experience had been so negative.

Week nine is the final teaching session and this is centered on looking at celebration. It is important that faith and spirituality is not the final night; week nine's topic allows for a wrap-up of the whole course experience. This session speaks to the fact that often people miss moments to celebrate, and are constantly waiting for life to be right, or better, or to have more time. This session encourages the participants to look for opportunities in their lives to celebrate.

Thus the final night is a night of celebration. The students are encouraged to use any creative form of painting that they have enjoyed and paint in the theme of celebration. They are shown a color wheel and taught about complimentary colors. The painting is part of the celebration of completion of the course and their painting is done to reflect this. By the time the course is completed the participant should have an idea of the fundamentals of painting and be able to produce some basic works.

In the small group on this final painting night, the participants look back in their journals to see what they wrote the first week about what they hoped to get out of the course. This is a very positive night, and I do not think that there has ever been a case in which none of the goals were reached. They are then encouraged to identify some things in their lives that they can celebrate and to look at what is stopping them from celebrating these things. The final question in the group is: What are your plans/strategies to keep going on the journey you have commenced through the Art and Soul course, both artistically and emotionally?

A wine and cheese night exhibiting the artwork from Art and Soul is a celebration of what has occurred. Celebration is a large part of the course. Often people feel their life is completely bad. The question asked during the course is: Is it all bad? The art exhibition is designed as a milestone of achievement and celebration of their work and growing painting ability. The exhibition allows participants an opportunity to show the work they have accomplished and several participants are selected to share their story and their experience of the Art and Soul course. This creates place for them to verbalize what occurred in their lives over the previous ten weeks. Family, friends, guests and other community members are invited to be a part of the evening. Several of these usually sign up for the following course.

At the end of the Art and Soul course students are invited to attend Kaleidoscope and continue to paint. They are also given the option to participate in the second initiative, Art for Justice, and to paint at the market. There are also several one-day Art and Soul courses throughout the year that they are invited to be a part of with students from previous Art and Soul courses. We have also introduced a monthly painting night that is run in a similar style to the Art and Soul course.

Rudy was a participant in the first Art and Soul course. He was the only student that had any painting experience. His wife had passed away three years earlier and he had not picked up a paintbrush since the day she died. Each week Rudy's paintings improved. About two months after the course, Rudy invited us to his home to see his paintings. He said that he did not know where he would be if not for Art and Soul. He has since invited us to two openings of his own personal art exhibitions in the city of Melbourne. At each of these he has insisted that we be in the opening photograph with him, stating that he would not have been able to do this without Art and Soul. Rudy has since helped out at Art and Soul, assisting with teaching painting at the classes.

8

Art and Soul: Connecting
with the Community

In the Community

BECAUSE OF THE SUCCESS with Art and Soul we have been invited
to run this course in many different areas. The only thing that
seems to be limiting it is our imagination. There are many opportunities for art to be used to impact those within our communities.
It opens up amazing opportunities for us to speak into the lives of
others. This chapter will detail some of the spin-offs from Art and
Soul that we have been able to run.

Children Suffering Anxiety

We were invited to run a group for children suffering from anxiety. This played out in the children refusing to go to school. I am
discovering that this is quite a common occurrence. We initially
ran the first course with eleven children from a primary school.
They were all different ages and class levels. I modified the session on identity for this group making it child friendly. We took
the children through a simple tonal painting with complimentary

colors. The children closed their eyes and used charcoal to draw intersecting lines on their canvas. They then painted the shapes different shades of one color. When the base dried they painted over the top of these shapes with a complimentary color. These children loved the painting process.

At the end of the painting we moved into our discussion phase. I spoke to the children about how difficult I had found school. I related how I had struggled to discover what I was good at. That I was constantly in trouble when I was at school and thought that I was just a bad kid. I struggled on many levels at school. The kids were very open.

I asked them to stretch their arm out and put their thumb up and then to close one eye. They were to cover another child's face with their thumb at a distance. As they did this they saw a giant thumb. Their thumb covered the whole face of another child opposite them. I asked them what was bigger, their thumb, or the other child's face. When we focus on the small negative things in our lives, sometimes they seem so much bigger to us than they really are. Many of the children began to talk about issues of being bullied at school.

At the end of the class the caseworkers took the children out to lunch and to a movie. When they returned home they reported that the most fun part of the day was the painting, and they related the story of the giant thumb. This surprised the social workers in that they related not only the painting experience but also the insights that they had learned.

We have since been invited to run this as a six-week program for these children. I have just finished writing three children's books to cover different issues that children face. The stories are on anger, in which I encourage the children to recognize the signs of anger in themselves as it occurs. The second book and session is on change, the purpose is to assist them to realize that change is a natural part of life, but we highlight that some things remain consistent. The third one is called "I am invisible until I'm naughty." In this session we help them to focus on the positive things in their lives. I am in the process of illustrating these books.

We will use the stories as a base for our teaching sessions, helping them to understand that issues such as anger and change are normal, but we need to learn how to deal with them. The painting sessions will give them the opportunit y to quietly process the information. The small group discussion and questions will be facilitated by the caseworkers. The children will be encouraged to explore their feelings and issues around their experiences. The idea is to help the children identify and then give them a plan to help them move forward.

Children respond really well to painting with fewer inhibitions than adults. Recently, at our annual Christmas street party that we hold in our neighborhood, I conducted a chalk-drawing competition on the pavement outside of our houses for the children. The children loved this. We have organized for them to come to my home for a painting session during the next school holidays.

Children with Autism

Jenny and I have also run a pilot program for children with autism. I told these children a story about a child feeling small and insignificant. We then took the children for a walk in the garden, looking at God's amazing creation. We asked them to crouch down or lay on the ground and look up and get a bug's-eye view of the world. We picked a few flowers and took them back and they painted a garden from the view of a bug. The last thing we put into their garden painting was the bug. These children responded really well to this session.

"At-Risk" Teenagers and Their Parents

The "At-Risk" teenager and parent class has been one of my favorite groups. We were invited by one of the local welfare agencies to work with a group of teenagers and a parent. The group consists entirely of "at-risk" teens. These sessions have been quite powerful. I have been really touched by some of the outcomes.

In the first session we adapted the identity session to suit them. Again, we did a tonal painting. We mixed up five shades in several different colors. Each participant took a palette and we tried to match up complimentary colors within the families so that they would produce matching paintings.

One of the participants was a single mother with two teenage boys, one sixteen and one twelve. The sixteen-year-old did not want to be there. He kept walking past his younger brother and punching him on the arm. He was slapping paint on his canvas and mostly looking bored and being quite disruptive as he annoyed his younger brother. We then used masking tape to apply strips across the painting and they began to paint over the top of the tape. Again, he was slapping the paint on. When we pulled the tape off, his face changed. He got a glimpse of what the painting could be. He re-taped his painting this time with considerable intention. Each of the next phases he began to get more excited by what he could see.

This session was finished with each person writing down three of their strengths and three of their weaknesses. They were then required to write down three strengths of the other members in their family. The sixteen-year-old boy was now quite positive in the group time. The twelve-year-old became a little emotional and the mother quite teary as they read what the older one had written about his younger brother; they stated that they had never heard the sixteen-year-old say anything positive to him. This was a really powerful moment. We may not have talked about Jesus openly, but I strongly felt Jesus present at that time.

We stuck the sheet with the three strengths that they had seen in themselves as well as the strengths that their family members had seen in them behind the painting as a reminder of the positive attributes that they have. When they look at the matching paintings on their wall at home, they will remember not only the family bonding of the painting experience, but it will also be a reminder of the positive qualities that other family members saw in them. The sixteen-year-old boy was asking how long until he could come back and do another painting session with us.

Since the spate of teenage suicides in my local community, one of the local high schools invited us to run a session with eight teenagers suffering depression. We are now planning to run a six-week program in 2014 with this same group.

Art Mentoring Program for "At-Risk" Teenagers

I am also currently planning a six-month intensive art mentoring program for twelve teenagers who are "at risk," teaching them to paint as well as mentoring them in life skills. For four hours per week this group will meet and will be taught to paint. Each teenager will also be assigned a general mentor from the Kaleidoscope community, to talk with them about life and to take an interest in them. This is a naturally evolving relationship where hopefully issues of faith and core beliefs will be discussed.

We will conduct three major projects during the six-month period. This is to display their growing skills, but also to sow into the confidence of the students and to showcase their artwork. The first one will be conducted two months into the program. The participants will create a concrete chalk art display. This will be held in one of the local schools. The students will be taken into the school, where they will spend the day working on their art pieces. The students at the college can view the artwork during lunch break. This is designed to be a positive peer experience for the participants.

The second project will be held at the four-month time frame. They will work on some graffiti-style street art. They will be tutored in this style of art and encouraged to find their style and also to paint an art piece that conveys a message that is meaningful to them.

The program will culminate in the students painting a large community mural in the City of Casey that tells their stories. This would be a great help to the well-being of the participants to be able to tell their stories as well as be an artistic gift to the local community.

Art and Soul for Traumatized Families

Last year I was invited by a local welfare agency to run an Art and Soul program with a traumatized family. The family consisted of a single mother, a twelve-year-old daughter and a fourteen-year-old son. They had suffered systematic abuse and were quite affected by it. At first I refused to run the group, as I felt a little out of my depth. The caseworker kept asking me to run it, as she felt that there were not a lot of options of programs for them.

After speaking to her several times I agreed to run it, on the proviso that she also participate in the course and lead the group discussions. I wrote an eight-week program for the family addressing issues including identity, loss and grief, shame, shifting paradigms, and faith and spirituality, among other themes.

Initially the children were uninterested in the teaching sessions, but mostly enjoyed the painting. As the weeks went on they became more and more interested in the teaching and engaged so much more. On the final session the children were asking their mother to be quiet so that they could listen. It was such a shift from week one to week eight. This was a really positive experience.

We concluded this group with an art exhibition. They invited family, friends, school teachers, as well as case workers from the welfare agency. The agency also invited the regional managers to attend. It was a great night as we displayed their work. At the end of the program they invited us to run the program again, this time with four families with their four caseworkers. We will commence this early next semester.

Art and Soul in the Chicago Prison

Possibly the most impacting experience that I have had with Art and Soul was with a group of inmates in a prison in Chicago. I conducted a six-day project with nine inmates. This was such a moving experience. I have been deeply impacted by my time in the prison. It actually took me about three weeks to be able to process what occurred and to be able to speak of it.

Michael Leshon is the chaplain at Metropolitan Correctional Center (MCC Chicago). He is currently writing his doctorate project through Fuller. His project topic is on reconciliation.[1] In his thesis he looks at four areas: Reconciliation with Self; Reconciliation with God; Reconciliation with Family; and Reconciliation with Community. Mike and I spent several months developing an Art and Soul program as a part of his project that would work to impact the inmates before release. My husband, Mick, Mike Leshon and I introduced the first part of the course, and Mike continued to run it for another ten weeks to complete his program.

I recall that just prior to leading the first session, we were covering the theme of identity, and I talked with Mike about how the program would run. I would teach the session on identity, taking the inmates through a painting process. They were going to paint a sepia tonal painting. This was to be followed by a small group conversation. Mike looked at me and explained that these men were not going to share anything in a small group. He continued that it was important for me to realize that anything that they shared in a group could be used against them. He reiterated that they were not going to engage on that level. This made so much sense; I just had not taken that into consideration when planning for it. I quickly decided that instead of getting them to share with one another, I would ask them to reflect in their visual diaries. And so we commenced. The session was reasonable, but far from the best one that I had run.

At the end of the session, Mike told me that I needed to share more of my own story. The next session was on reconciliation with God. In this session I shared my journey of faith, which included being set free from drug addiction and finding Jesus. I told the men how confusing the journey of finding God was for me, as well as telling some amusing stories from my past. They began to warm to me. In this session we did another tonal painting, this time an abstract in complimentary colors. Again they used their visual diary for their personal reflections.

---

1. Mike welcomes further inquiries into this project. He can be contacted at mleshon@bop.gov or slleshon@aol.com.

The following session was where it all began to gel for the men, and I guess for myself. This session was conducted in a small room in the basement gym. As an outsider, it seems to be a fairly big deal moving the prisoners from one section of the prison to another. The basement is an exercise room, set up as a basketball court; there are several small rooms on one side of the court. This is where we conducted some of the sessions. The third session was on reconciliation with family, and I decided to do a session on shame.

The teaching informed them that guilt is concerned with what we have done. Shame is about who we are. The painting for this one was on *The Red Tree*, by Shaun Tan. Four of the inmates painted the same picture: a person trapped inside a bottle. This was appropriate to how they felt and what they were experiencing.

I distributed a printed sheet on characteristics of shame and they were instructed to circle any of the characteristics that applied to them. One of the younger men looked at me and said, "What do you mean circle any?" The whole list applies to me. He looked at the other inmates and questioned, "This list pretty well describes who we are, doesn't it?" At that point something shifted and they began to share a lot more freely than they had previously.

At the end of the session, I walked out into the basement. In the meantime, about thirty other men had been brought down from another floor and were exercising. I began to walk over to the other side of the court to wait at the door to the stairwell, which was locked. Mike and Mick were still gathering the painting equipment and cleaning up from class. I looked up at all of these men exercising quite strenuously, and was thinking, wow, this is like a movie. And then suddenly the thought dawned on me: this is not a movie. This is real life. Here I was the only female in the room with a group of inmates quite actively working out. As the realization hit me, I became a little overwhelmed and maybe a little frightened. I looked up to find a group of inmates from the painting group walking up and surrounding me as I walked to the other side of the basement. I was really touched by this and found it quite overwhelming. There was a connection for me from that point onward.

Something had happened for me and for the men in this session. The following session was on reconciliation with family. I was teaching on connections with others. I talked about how that to really reach our potential we need connection with others. On our own we can achieve a certain amount of success, but to excel we need others. We talked about relationships and codependency, dependency, interdependency.

The painting exercise for this session was portrait painting. These are in abstract form. The inmates began by standing together and holding their canvases next to one another. They drew a pencil line through their canvas, joining up with the people on either side of them. This line eventually became a rope connecting each painting to another one. The background was painted green and the rope painted red. The portrait was painted on top of the rope, with the sides of the rope left clear to join up with a painting on either side. This was quite a powerful exercise.

At the end of the session the men stood side by side, holding their paintings up and allowing the rope to connect them. Their paintings were really good. I reflected on how each painting was quite good on its own, but together it was a really powerful display. And that is what it is like being in community. Together we are better. I called one of them forward to look at what they had created together. Seeing them together was quite meaningful. I called another man out to have a look. This continued on as one by one they all would jump out of the line to look at the community of paintings and then move back to hold one another's work. It was quite a profound moment. We talked about the need for us to be in community.

Mike Leshon led the next session on Reconciliation with Self, in which I assisted. His teaching session was quite powerful as he spoke on Israel's incarceration in Egypt and the affect that this had on them as a people. I hadn't really thought through the implications of the painting session, but it was quite humorous as we got into it. I had decided to paint the background in a dusky blue and the men drew an outline of their hands. They were then to paint their handprints in a cobalt blue.

I mixed up several warm shades of pinks, reds and oranges and talked about the uniqueness of every individual and how life experience affects us. They were then encouraged to use their fingers and put their finger prints all over the painting. One of them began to laugh about finger prints being taken. I had not realized the implications. At this point I told them that if they were uncomfortable doing that they could use an implement to complete the painting. They all laughed and said that the bureau had all of their fingerprints and DNA anyway, so it wouldn't matter. This was a really light moment, which helped in the bonding and moving forward of the group.

Mike then led the group discussion concerning the affects that incarceration has on a person. He gave them a list of these effects, which included lack of trust and an inhibited sense of exploration. For example, if I walked up to a door that was closed, I might try to open the door, but the effect that institutionalization has is that these men would stand and wait. He talked about how since they were incarcerated they would close off a part of their emotions to protect themselves. He continued that this switch would not easily reconnect, so the implications for their families and those in relationship where quite significant. One of the inmates was quite surprised at the list that was written up. He asked what could be done to help them. It was quite confronting for them as they began their discussion time. The discussion led to deeper conversation than had been experienced in the previous group time.

The final session in which I was involved was the second one in the Reconciliation with God series. Again Mike and I shared the facilitation of this group. Mike began teaching on the helplessness of our situation and how God initiates reconciliation. We only need to respond. We may lay down our life for a friend, but Jesus laid down his life for us while we were estranged from him. He made reference to Paul and how he was reconciled to Jesus even after the persecution and murder of his soon-to-be brothers in Christ. Mike talked about how we allow guilt to get in the way of reconciliation and the need to move beyond this. For the painting exercise, we created a small collage on a canvas board. We used a light wash rather than thick paint and glued sheet music on the board creating patterns and pictures and then highlighted areas and painted symbols onto the board. Words were highlighted or written on the top of the work.

For the small group time I decided to lead the men in a spiritual meditation. I asked them to close their eyes and to imagine themselves in the picture that I would paint. I spoke of them being outside on a beautiful clear day. The sky overhead was a beautiful clear blue. In front of them was a large mountain range and just before them was a lake. I asked them to settle themselves down and lean back against a tree. As they sat, the sky began to change and the colors of orange and purple began to appear as the sun began to recede. They could hear the birds begin to sing their nighttime symphony. And to their left in the bushes they could hear the rustle of the animals beginning to stir for their nighttime activities.

As I watched their faces relax into this beautiful picture, I then asked them, "Where is Jesus right at this moment? In this place with you, where is he?" After several minutes I called them back to the present moment. I asked if any of them wanted to share where Jesus had been for them. One man related that he was right beside him. Another agreed, yes, Jesus was sitting right next to him sharing the beautiful sunset with him. Another said that initially he was behind the tree and then walked around from behind and knelt in front of him.

Then one man became quite agitated and said, "He was somewhere I didn't want him to be. I didn't want him to be there." I was thinking where on earth could Jesus be with this man. Others continued to share where he was for them, with this man continuing to be rather agitated. At the end of the session he came up to me and asked if I wanted to read his journal. I was quite surprised at this because his journal was a very personal thing. I read what he had written. Then he asked if I wanted to know where Jesus was for him in the meditation. By this stage I was dying to know where he could be. He pounded on his chest. He was in here. I didn't want him there, but he was in here. I told him that Jesus wanted to be a part of his life and that this was a good thing. He reiterated that he did not want him to be there. He told me that he had a wound on his heel that would not heal. It was a wound from where he had been shot. I told him that maybe God wanted to heal him. He replied that he did not want to be healed, that he had been shot because he was so arrogant. His friend had been shot and killed because he was so arrogant. This was a really powerful moment, and I was overcome with tears at this point. I reconfirmed that God wanted to be a part of that.

The same man began to speak to Mike about how Mike had really impacted him through the Reconciliation Course. He told Mike that he was extremely touched by what Mike was bringing into the prison. He said that it was fine for those that came and went (I was in that category), but Mike was opening himself up and sharing very deeply with these men in a way that was profoundly affecting them. This was really touching to be present as what had been shared in early sessions about shutting off emotions was being approached now in a totally different way.

Coming away from the prison that day was a very strange mix of emotions. On one hand I had seen God doing some amazing things over the previous six days. On the other, we were leaving and I was quite emotional. I remember saying that I could not believe how I was so deeply affected by nine inmates I had only known for six days and I would never see again. These sessions affected me deeply. Over the next ten weeks Michael Leshon continued to run the rest of the program. We had developed art programs and continued to work through discussion.

Later this year we will return to Chicago to run another Art and Soul reconciliation program in the prison. We are also looking at doing a workshop at a Salvation Army halfway house in Chicago. The final thing that we are looking to conduct is a community reentry program for ex-offenders. The plan is to work in a local community for several days with a group of ex-offenders and their partners. We will address several issues while teaching them to paint. The small group discussion will assist them to work through issues. It would be good to be able to set each family up with a painting kit so that they are able to continue painting as a family once the workshops are completed.

There is such a benefit in being able to teach and lead others in right-brain pursuits. Engaging in art assists the processing of information in a totally different way than many of the inmates are used to. The small group discussions become so much easier to conduct. We have been blessed to see this work on so many different levels.

Where to from Here?

Art and Soul with Those Rescued from Human Trafficking

I AM ON THE board of an anti-human trafficking organization called Abolishion. This organization operates in Europe and mainly focuses in Romania and Moldova, although it is based in Paris. In 2015 we are planning on setting up an Art and Soul program for the girls that have been rescued. In 2014 we will go over to Romania and spend a couple of weeks looking at the work that is being done and begin to plan how to go about setting up the program. This is a huge problem in our world and removing the girls from sex slavery is just a small part of the need that exists. I know art can bring relief and can begin to point toward healing. I pray that Jesus is able to meet them at this point and bring some sort of reconciliation to their lives.

Art and Soul for Refugees

A few years ago a lovely lady who worked at the local council did the Art and Soul course. She worked with people who were unemployed. She invited us to run a course that would give them some self-confidence. When we ran the course the participants were nearly all immigrants. This stirred my heart as I connected with a group of Muslim women from various countries.

Recently we were invited to create an Art and Soul course for refugees. This will commence in February 2014. I am currently writing a ten-week program that will hopefully look at some of the issues that the refugees may face—for example, change, difference, value of culture. The people attending the course have the most incredible stories of loss, violence, and fear. Most of the participants in the initial course are from Middle Eastern countries such as Afghanistan and Iran. I am challenged by the issues that these people face, not only in their horror stories of leaving their homeland, but in their stories of arrival, stories of suspicion and disrespect. I am praying for Jesus to reveal himself in these classes and to be able to be a light and voice in a very difficult place.

Portraits of Local People in My Community

I am currently working toward the painting project mentioned in chapter 1: painting random people that I meet in my local community. I have almost completed Wendy's painting and am currently working on my second portrait. David is from the Oromo region of Ethiopia. He told me of watching horrific acts of violence occur to his family before he escaped to Australia. He loves his new country, but his heart breaks for the atrocities that have occurred, and continue to occur, in his homeland. He is so grateful that someone is listening and willing to tell his story. As I engage at this level with the people that I meet in my community I am in awe and inspired by God's creation, the imago Dei, and the value that he places in each one. I feel extremely privileged to be able to connect on this level very quickly with these people.

As I look back over what God has done through Art for Justice, Art and Soul, and other painting projects, I realize that we are only limited by how far our imagination extends. God wants us to get out of our church buildings and our narrow norms and touch those who are living around us. Whether this is by something as simple as having a chalk art competition for the neighborhood kids or running an art program for refugees or sex-trafficked women, God is present.

Often when we look at something that has taken years to develop it seems that it may be too difficult or too far out of reach, but beginning small is the key. I would encourage you to connect with other artists. Who are the other artists that you know? Maybe they are more art lovers than accomplished artists. It is not important that they are professional or perfected artists. Get some butcher paper and brainstorm the opportunities that you have. Who are the people in your world? The artists, art lovers, people connectors. Can you gather them together and share some thoughts and ideas? Where are you intersecting the community outside of the church? Begin to dream of the possibilities. Start small, start simple, but start something.

Bibliography

Abolishion. Anti-human trafficking organization operating in Romania and Moldova. http://www.abolishion.org.

Andrews, Gavin, et al. *The Mental Health of Australians*. Canberra: Mental Health Branch, Commonwealth Department of Health and Aged Care, 1999.

Art and Soul. Course that uses art to explore some of the emotional responses and thinking that lead to depression, anxiety, and loneliness. www.artandsoul.org.au.

Australian Bureau of Statistics. "2011 Census Quick Stats: Greater Melbourne." http://www.abs.gov.au/websitedbs/censushome.nsf/home/data.

Australian Bureau of Statistics. "Year Book Australia, 2004." http://www.abs.gov.au/ausstats/abs@.nsf/0/E6AFF66C68CED997CA256DEA000539D6?opendocument.

Australian Department of Foreign Affairs and Trade. "Sport Performance and Participation." http://www.health.gov.au/internet/budget/publishing.nsf/Content/2009-2010_Health_PBS_sup2/$File/Outcome%2015%20-%20Sport%20Performance%20and%20Participation.pdf.

Australian Department of Health. "What Is an Anxiety Disorder?" Mental Health and Workforce Division. May 2007. http://www.health.gov.au/internet/main/publishing.nsf/Content/6E02F4C9EA81857FCA257BF00 0212085/$File/whatanx2.pdf.

Australian Sociological Association. "Church Attendance Falling." Media release, June 19, 2002. http://staging.tasa.org.au/publications/church-attendance-falling.

Barna, George. *Grow Your Church from the Outside*. Ventura, CA: Regal, 2002.

Barrett, David B., et al. *World Christian Encyclopedia*. Oxford: Oxford University Press, 2001.

Baudrillard, Jean. *Revenge of the Crystal*. Edited and translated by Paul Foss and Julian Pefanis. Sydney: Pluto, 1990.

83

Bibliography

Bosch, David J. *Transforming Mission: Paradigm Shifts in Theology of Mission.* Maryknoll: Orbis, 1991.

Bouma, Gary D. *Australian Soul: Religion and Spirituality in the Twenty-First Century.* Melbourne: Cambridge University Press, 2006.

Brueggemann, Walter. *Theology of the Old Testament.* Minneapolis: Fortress, 1997.

Calver, Clive. "Postmodernism: An Evangelical Blind Spot?" *Evangelical Missions Quarterly* 35 (1999) 430–34.

Calvin, John. *Institutes of the Christian Religion.* Vol. 1. Grand Rapids: Eerdmans, 1957.

Cameron, Julia. *The Artist's Way: Discovering and Recovering Your Creative Self.* London: Pan, 1997.

Campbell, Jonathan. "Postmodernism: Ripe for a Global Harvest—But Is the Church Ready?" *Evangelical Missions Quarterly* 35 (1999) 432–38.

Carson, D. A. *Becoming Conversant with the Emerging Church.* Grand Rapids: Zondervan, 2005.

"Convict Artists in Governor Macquarie's Era." State Library of New South Wales. Discover Collections. History of Our Nation. http://www.sl.nsw.gov.au/discover_collections/history_nation/macquarie/artists.

Csikszentmihalyi, Mihaly. *Flow: The Psychology of Optimal Experience.* New York: Harper & Row, 1990.

DeConcini, Barbara. "The Crisis of Meaning in Religion and Art." *Christian Century*, March 20–27, 1991. http://www.religion-online.org/showarticle.asp?title=174.

Detweiler, Craig. *Purple State of Mind: Finding Middle Ground in a Divided Culture.* Eugene, OR: Harvest House, 2008.

"Dreaming and the Dreamtime." AboriginalArtOnline.com. http://www.aboriginalartonline.com/culture/dreaming.php.

Dyrness, William A. *Senses of the Soul: Art and the Visual in Christian Worship.* Eugene, OR: Cascade, 2008.

Egan, Kieran. *Imagination in Teaching and Learning: The Middle School Years.* Chicago: University of Chicago Press, 1992.

Evans, Graeme. "Measure for Measure: The Evidence Of Culture's Contribution to Regeneration." *Urban Studies* 42 (2005) 959–83.

Evans, Megan. "Opportunities and Challenges for Artists." *Artwork* 39 (1998) 6–9.

Fee, Gordon D., and Douglas K. Stuart. *How to Read the Bible for All Its Worth.* Grand Rapids: Zondervan, 1993.

Fiddes, Paul S. *Participating in God: A Pastoral Doctrine of the Trinity.* Louisville: Westminster John Knox, 2000.

Flynn, Hazel. "Home Ownership Dream Fading For Generation Y." Lifestyle. *Yahoo.com*, August 29, 2013. https://au.lifestyle.yahoo.com/marie-claire/news-and-views/latest/a/18702716/home-ownership-dream-fading-for-generation-y.

Frankl, Viktor E. *Man's Searching for Meaning*. New York: Washington Square, 1963.

Freddoso, Alfred J. "The Church and Art." With excerpt from Pope John Paul's *Letter to Artists* (April 4, 1999). *Logos* 5 (2002) 217–20. http://www3.nd.edu/~afreddos/papers/jpii-artists.htm.

Fretheim, Terence E. *God and World in the Old Testament: A Relational Theology of Creation*. Nashville: Abingdon, 2005.

Fundraising Institute Australia. "2012 Giving Trends Report." August 6, 2013. http://www.fia.org.au/news.php/182/2012-giving-trends-report-released.

GraceWorks Myanmar. A faith-based community development organization. http://www.graceworksmyanmar.org.au.

Grenz, Stanley J. *A Primer on Postmodernism*. Grand Rapids: Eerdmans, 1996.

———. *Theology for the Community of God*. Grand Rapids: Eerdmans, 1994.

Guder, Darrell L. *Missional Church: A Vision for the Sending of the Church in North America*. Grand Rapids: Eerdmans, 1998.

Halley, Henry H. *Halley's Bible Handbook*. Grand Rapids: Zondervan, 1965.

Hauerwas, Stanley. *Performing the Faith*. Grand Rapids: Brazos, 2004.

Harbinson, Colin. "Restoring the Arts to the Church: The Role of Creativity in the Expression of Truth." International Christian Dance Fellowship. Edited from a chapter in *The Complete Evangelism Guidebook*, edited by Scott Dawson. Grand Rapids: Baker, 2006. http://www.icdf.com/restoring-the-arts-to-the-church.php.

Hicks, Mack R. "Who Stole the Right Side of Your Brain? Grinch—or Santa?" *Psychology Today*, December 30, 2013. http://www.psychologytoday.com/blog/digital-pandemic/201312/who-stole-the-right-side-your-brain-grinch-or-santa.

Hirsch, Alan. *The Forgotten Ways: Reactivating the Missional Church*. Grand Rapids: Brazos, 2006.

———. *The Forgotten Ways Handbook*. With Darryn Altclass. Grand Rapids: Brazos, 2009.

Hirsch, Alan, and Debra Hirsch. *Untamed: Reactivating a Missional Form of Discipleship*. Grand Rapids: Baker, 2010.

Holden, John. "How We Value Arts and Culture." *Asia Pacific Journal of Arts and Cultural Management* 6 (2009) 447–56.

Horton, Stanley M. *Systematic Theology*. Springfield, MO: Logion, 1995.

Johnson, Louise. "Valuing Arts and Culture in the Community." *Asia Pacific Journal of Arts and Cultural Management* 6 (2009) 471–87.

Kitchener, Betty, and Anthony Jorm. *Youth Mental Health First Aid: A Manual for Adults Assisting Youth*. Melbourne: University of Melbourne: 2009.

Luther, Martin. "An Open Letter to the Christian Nobility of the German Nation Concerning the Reform of the Christian Estate, 1520." From *Works of Martin Luther: With Introductions and Notes*, vol. 2. Philadelphia: Holman, 1915. http://www.iclnet.org/pub/resources/text/wittenberg/luther/web/nblty-01.html.

Maxwell, Ian, and Fiona Winning. "Towards a Critical Practice: A Model for Talking and Writing about Community Art Works." *Artwork* 49 (2001) 8–20.

McCallum, Dennis. "Recent Research Indicating Decline in the Western Evangelical Church." *Xenos.org.* http://www.xenos.org/books/satan/churchdecline.htm.

McKnight, Scot. *Community Called Atonement.* Nashville: Abingdon, 2007.

McKnight, Scot, et al. *Church in the Present Tense: A Candid Look at What's Emerging.* Grand Rapids: Brazos, 2011.

McLaren, Brian D. *Everything Must Change: Jesus, Global Crises and the Revolution of Hope.* Nashville: Nelson, 2007.

McNeal, Reggie. *Missional Renaissance: Changing the Scorecard for the Church.* San Francisco: Jossey-Bass, 2009.

———. *The Present Future: Six Tough Questions for the Church.* San Francisco: Jossey-Bass, 2003.

Mennekes, Friedhelm. "The Art of Spirituality." Interview by Donna Noble, *Eureka Street,* June 16, 2006. http://www.eurekastreet.com.au/article.aspx?aeid=1091.

Michelle Sanders. Artist's website. www.michellesanders.com.au.

National Church Life Survey (NCLS) Research. "National Church Life Survey 2011." http://www.ncls.org.au.

Operation Hope. http://operationhopeinc.org.au/sisteract.

Park, Vivian S. "Scholars Find Decline of Christianity in the West." *Christian Post,* March 6, 2004. http://www.christianpost.com/news/scholars-find-decline-of-christianity-in-the-west-19971.

Passmore, Daryl. "We Believe in Easter, but We Mistrust Church." *Melbourne Herald Sun,* April 8, 2012.

Presser, Stanley, and Linda Stinson. "Data Collection Mode and Social Desirability Bias in Self-Reported Religious Attendance." *American Sociological Review* 63 (1998) 137–45. http://www.jstor.org/stable/2657486.

Reid, Alvin. *Radically Unchurched: Who They Are and How to Reach Them.* Grand Rapids: Kregel, 2002

Rock, David. "Stop Trying to Solve Problems." *Psychology Today,* September 18, 2012. http://www.psychologytoday.com/blog/your-brain-work/201209/stop-trying-solve-problems.

Sanders, Van. "The Mission of God and the Local Church." Chapter 2 in *Pursuing the Mission of God in Church Planting,* compiled by John M. Bailey. Alpharetta, GA: North American Mission Board, SBC, 2006.

Sayers, Dorothy. *Christian Letters to a Post-Christian World: A Selection of Essays.* Grand Rapids: Eerdmans, 1969.

Shaw, Luci. "Art and Christian Spirituality: Companions in the Way." *Direction* 27 (1998) 109–22. http://www.directionjournal.org/article/?980.

Stafford, Eve. "CCD—Why Do We Do It?" *Artwork* 39 (1998) 16–20.

Strong, James. *Strong's Exhaustive Concordance Complete and Unabridged.* Grand Rapids: Baker, 1980.

Sweet, Leonard. *I Am a Follower: The Way, Truth, and Life of Following Jesus.* Nashville: Nelson, 2012.

Tan, Shaun. *The Red Tree.* Sydney: Lothian Children's, 2001

Thwaites, James. *The Church beyond the Congregation: The Strategic Role of the Church in the Postmodern Era.* Carlisle, UK: Paternoster, 2001.

Turner, Steve. *Imagine: A Vision for Christians in the Arts.* Downers Grove: InterVarsity, 2001.

Vine, W. E., et al. *Vine's Complete Expository Dictionary of Old and New Testament Words.* Nashville: Nelson, 1985.

Ware, Vicki-Ann. Qualitative research evaluation of Art and Soul. Unpublished report. Melbourne, 2012.

Webber, Robert E. *Ancient-Future Evangelism: Making Your Church a Faith-Forming Community.* Grand Rapids: Baker, 2007.

Wright, N. T. *The New Testament and the People of God.* Minneapolis: Fortress, 1992.

Lightning Source UK Ltd.
Milton Keynes UK